Praise for

# FROM CLUTTER TO CLARITY

"Having long agreed with the German saying that 'order is half of life,' this brilliantly insightful book will help anyone see that the tigers of clutter are only paper, dispense with the drama, and find true peace in all of its manifestations."

—**Mike Dooley**, *New York Times* best-selling author of *Infinite Possibilities*

"Get out your highlighter! Kerri's book will inspire and motivate you to make gigantic steps forward by addressing your clutter. When you change your clutter, you transform your life. With a depth of wisdom and practical, easy-to-understand tenets, *From Clutter to Clarity* will take you on a profound journey of inner exploration. Highly recommended!"

—**Denise Linn**, best-selling author of *Feng Shui for the Soul* and *Energy Strands*

"Phenomenal is an understatement! In *From Clutter to Clarity*, Kerri takes you on a fun and fascinating journey behind the thoughts, things, and people that are cluttering your ability to renew, heal, and create reserves of energy and peace in your life. If you're ready to accelerate opening up untapped potential, buy this smart and no-nonsense book!"

—**Janine Driver**, *New York Times* best-selling author of *You Say More Than You Think* and CEO of Body Language Institute

# FROM
# CLUTTER
# TO CLARITY

## ALSO BY KERRI RICHARDSON

*What Your Clutter Is Trying to Tell You*

All of the above are available at your local bookstore,
or may be ordered by visiting:

Hay House USA: www.hayhouse.com®
Hay House Australia: www.hayhouse.com.au
Hay House UK: www.hayhouse.co.uk
Hay House India: www.hayhouse.co.in

—•—

# FROM
# CLUTTER
# TO CLARITY

## CLEAN UP YOUR
## MINDSET TO CLEAR OUT
## YOUR CLUTTER

## KERRI RICHARDSON

**HAY HOUSE, INC.**
Carlsbad, California • New York City
London • Sydney • New Delhi

*Published in the United States by:* Hay House, Inc.: www.hayhouse
.com® • *Published in Australia by:* Hay House Australia Pty. Ltd.: www
.hayhouse.com.au • *Published in the United Kingdom by:* Hay House UK,
Ltd.: www.hayhouse.co.uk • *Published in India by:* Hay House Publishers
India: www.hayhouse.co.in

*Cover design:* Mary Ann Smith • *Interior design:* Nick C. Welch

Cataloging-in-Publication Data is on file at the Library of Congress

Tradepaper ISBN: 978-1-4019-6014-8
E-book ISBN: 978-1-4019-6015-5
Audiobook ISBN: 978-1-4019-6064-3

11  10  9  8  7  6  5  4  3  2
1st edition, December 2020

Printed in the United States of America

*To my Mama, for being a loving and compassionate role model, for cheering me along when the doubts crept in, and for finally admitting that I am, in fact, the best of seven.* 😊

# CONTENTS

# INTRODUCTION

When Melissa and I decided to live in a tiny house (yes, like the ones you see on reality television), I never anticipated the challenges that would come with such a significant downsize. I knew we'd have some tough decisions to make, but I couldn't have predicted the deep, emotional work that would be involved. However, it was that work that opened up our lives in the best way possible.

At the time of writing this, we have been living in our tiny house for 14 months. It's a comfortable 28 by 8.5 feet, about 240 square feet in total. It's a modern-style home on wheels that has everything we need: a fully functioning kitchen, living room/office, and bedroom loft. Our bathroom has a big, beautiful shower that might just be my favorite part of the whole place. It's small (tiny, if you will), but it's home.

Downsizing to this lifestyle was a four-year process. Our first house was 2,000 square feet and came with more rooms and storage space than we ever needed. After selling that, we moved into a 750-square-foot apartment, and then into one that was a mere 500 square feet, before settling into the tiny house. With each round of paring down, the task became more challenging. I found myself facing difficult decisions about what I should or shouldn't keep.

Do I keep my high school yearbook? How many spatulas do I really need? I love this dress that I wore to my niece's wedding, but will I ever wear it again? What about this waffle iron my mother-in-law gave me in honor of the special breakfast we had the morning after my wedding? Despite thinking we had finished simplifying, there were still many possibly superfluous things.

Why were some things so easy to let go of, while others caused me to spiral into speculation, question my character, or doubt my intuition? What was so important about all of this stuff? As I asked myself these questions, I realized that my struggle in deciding had little to do with the items themselves and everything to do with the meaning I had assigned to them.

Of course I should keep my yearbooks! That's something everyone hangs on to.

I'm an adult. Aren't I supposed to have at least a few spatulas? Just having one seems desperate and lacking.

I can't fit into that spring dress right now, but it sure is pretty. Remember how much thinner I was then?

My mother-in-law would be disappointed if I got rid of the waffle iron. She was so excited to give it to us. I don't want her to think I'm ungrateful.

It sounds silly now, but at the time, this is what was running through my head. I realized just how often our beliefs get in the way of decluttering. So I decided to take a new approach. Any time I wrestled with the decision to keep or donate, I worked on cleaning up my thoughts first. I'd reassure my younger self (she's the one who created these beliefs, after all) that nothing catastrophic would happen if I chose to do things my way.

It's okay to get rid of something that other people would keep.

I can thrive in abundance even with just one spatula.

I don't have to fit back into that dress again to be worthy.

My mother-in-law's love for me isn't conditional.

I realized it's also okay to keep things others would get rid of. After all, only I get to decide what is clutter to me and what isn't.

I had been convincing myself of those old ideas for years, so I knew it would take time to unlearn them. And, like going through everything I owned, it was a process. It took a lot of work. And then something cool happened.

I realized I wasn't just reframing my perspective about things. I was also learning about myself and how my mindset gets in the way as I pursue my dreams and goals. What a revelation to have while clearing clutter!

It wasn't easy to accept. Growing up, I learned that how you do anything is how you do everything. If I'm talking myself into keeping an extra spatula for fear of looking pathetic, then there's a good chance I'm doing (or not doing) something else for the same reason.

If I'm worried that donating a gift from my mother-in-law will change her opinion of me, I probably consider my other relationships transactional. That's certainly not ideal, but how can I change it? By using my clutter as a tool for transformation.

As you decide what to keep in your life and what to remove, whether it's thoughts, things, or people, pay attention to the stories you tell yourself. By doing so, you gain incredible insight into your belief system. It's this insight that will help you clear the real clutter and make moves on blazing the trail to your BHAG—your big, hairy, audacious goal.

Our best life didn't start the moment we moved into the tiny house, and the learning didn't stop either. It just showed itself differently. For example, I knew we'd have to get creative with storage and figure out how to do the galley kitchen dance, but I didn't think about just how "in your face" unfinished projects would be. Because clutter is amplified in such a small space, we quickly learned how to deal with all kinds of messes.

Although our kitchen is bigger than that of most Manhattan studios, the limited space doesn't allow for a full sink of dishes or ingredients left strewn about the counter. When I make a meal, I put things away as I prepare the dish instead of leaving them all out until the end. Melissa cleans up right after dinner because if there are dirty dishes in the house, we can see them from any angle. In 240 square feet, there's no such thing as "out of sight, out of mind."

These tight quarters also prompt quicker cleanup of communication-based messes. If Melissa and I are snapping at each other, there's nowhere to go without physically leaving the house. That's still an option if one of us needs space to process, but we've been much more mindful of communicating cleanly and clearly. Instead of making a snide comment like, "I guess I'll clean the cat box again," I speak to the source. "Can we take turns cleaning the cat box? I'm starting to feel resentful because I seem to be doing it a lot."

This requires an incredible amount of vulnerability because we go right to the heart of the matter instead of wasting time bitching about the superficial issue. We're certainly not perfect. We still gripe on occasion, but it's much shorter-lived. It has to be, since we're in such close quarters. That said, cleaning up messes sooner rather than later is a good practice in any home or any type of relationship.

With less, you feel lighter. Brighter. More alive. That isn't limited to physical clutter, either. Even if you have the shelves and drawers necessary for a lot of stuff, it doesn't mean you have the energetic capacity or mental bandwidth to manage it all. Watch out for the mindset that says, "have space, must fill," whether that applies to your home, head, or heart. It's okay to have space. I should know—even in my tiny home, I have some!

Despite us paring way down, Melissa and I have made plenty more donation runs since moving in. I'm sure it comes as no surprise that I love to get rid of the things I no longer need, love, or use. After all, if my space or energy is feeling crowded, it leaves me no space to energetically expand into.

Once I've created that space, I then do my best to be mindful of allowing only the thoughts, things, or people *deserving* of occupying a precious slot in my life. My space is sacred and not everyone or everything is worthy of being in it, so instead of buying things unconsciously or tolerating an unhealthy friendship, I do my best to evaluate what my life is comprised of. I encourage you to do the same. Because chances are, if you've read this far, you've got clutter too. *Everyone does.*

As if you don't feel overwhelmed enough, I've now made you think about even more clutter in your life! But this is good, I promise. I want you to see all obstacles as clutter so you know you can clear them. But I get it. You're aggravated. You're fed up. You're overwhelmed. Your clutter is draining you, physically, emotionally, and spiritually. You feel frozen and want so desperately to break free, but you can't seem to get yourself to do it. Why is that? Why is it so difficult to clean up your clutter?

Here's the thing: you're doing it all wrong. Thinking you simply need to set aside a weekend and knock it all out assumes that the only thing getting in your way is a lack of time. There's much more to it than that. And honestly, that's good news. Any failed attempts up until this point are not because you're lazy, messy, or unmotivated. It's because you're looking at the wrong kind of clutter. There's clutter under that clutter. There are fears, doubts, blocking beliefs, and more that are the true culprits in making it tough for you to break free. But this is where the deep clean comes in—the healing of the clutter within to clear the clutter on the outside. This is what we'll be doing together in these pages. Together, we will make it right by peeling back all the layers to be sure you're answering all the calls within.

The piles, stacks, and boxes will be the tools you'll use to gain the clarity you need to finally let them go. We'll explore, in depth, the three core causes of clutter, and when you understand which of the three are in play for you, you'll not only clear your physical space but you'll also heal aspects of your life you've likely struggled with for a long time. Like I said: everyone has clutter. And yours may be where you least expect it.

This book is divided into two parts. The first section dissects the three core causes of clutter and invites you to use them as excavators to uncover the roots of your clutter hotspots. The second section will take you into specific rooms and areas where clutter commonly accumulates to show you this process in action. By observing the roll-out of this unique approach, you will know precisely how to apply it to your own home and life.

Since you have this book in your hands, that also tells me you are a spiritual warrior. You are primed and ready for this mission. You are eager to break free from the limitations that surround you and finally claim the space in your life in which you can expand, grow, and live out loud.

In reading this book, you'll get to know yourself on a deep, intimate level. You'll come face-to-face with your resistance, your fear, your younger self, and your shadow self, and you'll learn how beneficial the relationships you have with them are in becoming the confident trailblazer you've longed to be.

In my first book, *What Your Clutter Is Trying to Tell You*, I introduced you to the concept of your clutter being more than just "stuff"; that there is a message in the mess.

Anything you resist clearing or letting go of has something to tell you. In this book, we're going to answer that call.

Whether you're looking to right-size your home and belongings, simplify your life, or unload your doubts and fears, this book will teach you the powerful and loving approach of using your clutter as a catalyst for change to propel you toward your goals.

Let's make some space for your new life, shall we?

## CHAPTER 1

# REDEFINING CLUTTER: THE SECRETS IN YOUR STUFF

The struggle with clutter is real. It seems to multiply daily and taunts you from the corners, closets, and counters. No matter how many pretty containers you buy or organizational shows you watch, you can't seem to get it in check.

We're going on a journey to places that will surprise you, challenge you, and ultimately, help you make space for new adventures and the incredible life that you've been dreaming of.

As we begin, I want you to forget everything you know about clutter. Forget any notion that it's just piles of stuff you've yet to sort through, or that the word *clutter* only pertains to physical items. I want you to see it as a catchall term that represents *anything that gets in the way of you living your most joyous and exuberant life*. It's a temper tantrum of your soul as it calls out to you for help. Your spirit desperately wants you to blaze your trail, but you first must bushwhack it and clear it of rubble and debris.

Clutter is a multifaceted, multilayered phenomenon that has little to do with you being disorganized and everything to do with the important role it plays in your life. If there are things, thoughts, or people in your life who don't contribute positively to or support your health and happiness, then you've got clutter.

There are two overarching categories of clutter: simple (which is easily cleared) and stubborn (which is, well, stubborn). Stubborn clutter is comprised of symptomatic clutter and core clutter. Remember this: Difficult-to-clear clutter is never about the stuff. It's about what the stuff represents.

We're approaching your clutter clearing from a soul- and heart-centered place. The work you are about to undertake involves much more than sorted clothes and filed paperwork. Will you clear physical clutter as a result of reading this book? Absolutely. Will you do it in the way you expect? Definitely not.

Whatever clutter you struggle with the most is where you'll find the most poignant learning opportunities about yourself, your values, and your mindset. The tactics you use to distract yourself or procrastinate give you a peek into the core causes of your clutter—what's *really* stopping you from clearing it.

In the chapters that follow, these tactics will be your tools for the messages in your messes. You'll use them to determine what layer of clutter you're facing (there are many) and how to clear it at the source. To clear stubborn clutter, you need to tend to your mindset before your behavior can change because it's there where the real blocks live.

## UNPACKING THE CONCEPT OF CLUTTER

When you think of clutter, stacks of paperwork, piles of clothes, or toys strewn about your family room probably come to mind.

But clutter comes in many forms. Despite the success with downsizing physical clutter that I shared earlier, I still have one hotspot that troubles me again and again. I've struggled to get rid of it for 30 years, and while I've had some success, it seems to inevitably return. My stubborn clutter hotspot? My weight. Yes, the pounds on my body.

I realize thinking of clutter as more than just "stuff" is pretty revolutionary, and a clutter revolution is just what you need! Approaching the removal of all kinds of clutter from a truly holistic place helps remove the shame related to it and allows you to see the intricacies in this multifaceted process.

There are three main categories of clutter, and each one is defined by how challenging it is to clear.

- **Simple Clutter:** If you're able to get rid of it without much effort, then it's *simple clutter*. Because there aren't hidden layers compounding this situation, clearing simple clutter is just a matter of making the time, committing to the task, and getting it done. For example, with my stubborn weight clutter, the *simple clutter* would be the pounds I can lose with little or minimal effort. They're not hanging on because of any bigger issue. By eating better and moving more, these pounds come off relatively easily.

- **Symptomatic Clutter:** If you struggle to make the time, make decisions, or let things go, you're dealing with *symptomatic clutter*. You're sure you're ready to let it go, but you can't seem to finish the job. Something is holding you back and you're not sure what. This is the most common kind of clutter and is an indication that something deeper and seemingly unrelated needs your attention.

With my stubborn hotspot, the *symptomatic clutter* is all the rest—the remaining pounds I struggle to lose or that come back again and again. Whether it's a plateau, a temptation to throw in the towel, or regaining some pounds, it is a tap on the shoulder that there's more work to do; that there are more layers to explore. It's those layers that will point to what's at the root of the struggle.

- **Core Clutter:** This represents those deeper issues that lie within or underneath the symptomatic clutter. This is the source of all other clutter and is the reason behind your inability to make progress. *Core clutter* is rarely, if ever, the first kind you identify. Simple or symptomatic clutter is what points you in this direction.

  Anytime you're feeling stuck, frustrated, or lost, there is core clutter in play. While this may seem intimidating, realizing that there is more going on is like picking up the shovel. You may not know what you're digging for, and that's okay. Just start digging. When you dive into the core clutter, I guarantee you that you will positively impact all areas of your life.

  When you sabotage your progress in any way, some part of you is benefitting from that stumble. If my expectations for weight loss are unrealistic, then my resistance is going to win. Maybe I'm using weight as armor to protect my sensitivity and vulnerability when what I really need to do is set some boundaries. Perhaps the pounds are validating a limiting belief that it's not safe to be thin. If any part of me believes I don't deserve to be treated well, I could be proving myself right by eating unhealthy foods.

The core clutter is the message in the mess. This is what is rumbling underneath stubborn clutter, and this is what your soul is asking you to work on to break free from the obstacles in your path.

## PAY ATTENTION TO THE CHATTER

"I'm such a procrastinator."
　　"How did I let it get this bad?"
　　"Where do I even begin?"
　　"I feel like I'm suffocating."
　　"I'm so overwhelmed."

Does any of this sound familiar? How often have you uttered those words or been disappointed in yourself for letting another day go by without doing what you said you were going to do? It's okay—it happens to everyone. But it's frustrating, isn't it? You so badly want to be free of the clutter and have the time and space to focus on far more important things like living in a space that nurtures you, finding deep and long-lasting love, growing your business, writing your book, inviting friends and family to visit, or whatever else living a full life means to you.

Think about the type of clutter you've found the most challenging. Maybe it's paperwork or books. It might be pounds on your body or a draining friendship. It could be the boxes and bins in your attic or garage. If the only thing stopping you from getting the job done is time and discipline, you'd have it handled. You may not enjoy it, but you'd likely have already made a dent in the job.

While it's nice to know the struggle isn't due to some character flaw, how does that knowledge help you make progress? For one, you can comfortably move past the chatter of your inner critic. You can dig beneath the simple clutter to get to the symptomatic and core clutter, which need clearing before the physical piles, draining relationships, or sabotaging thoughts will budge. This can take more work because symptomatic and core clutter are generally a lot more stubborn than, say, a stack of paper.

Over the years, I've discovered that, in my own life and in the lives of those I've worked with, the source of core clutter is any combination of three things: unrealistic expectations, limiting or old beliefs, and a lack of boundaries. Understanding which of these things is at the root of your struggles will help you better understand and ultimately clear the clutter in your life. As you investigate the message in your mess, you might find the cause to be one or a combination of the three. Because one cause often leads to another, you'll likely find more than one at work.

In the next three chapters, we'll dig deep into each cause and later apply this knowledge directly to your specific clutter to help you finally make the progress you've longed for.

## CHAPTER TAKEAWAYS

1. Clutter is anything that gets in the way of you living your best life. This can be thoughts, things, or people.

2. There are three types of clutter: simple, symptomatic, and core.

    a. Simple clutter is easy to let go of.
    b. Symptomatic clutter is what you want to let go of but struggle to do so. It has a message for you.
    c. Core clutter is the root cause beneath symptomatic clutter and is made up of limiting beliefs, a need for boundaries, and/or unrealistic expectations.

3. The clutter you struggle with the most offers you the deepest learning opportunities about yourself, your values, and your mindset.

## CHAPTER 2

# CORE CLUTTER CAUSE #1: UNREALISTIC EXPECTATIONS

Unrealistic expectations are often the biggest hurdles in any clutter-clearing endeavor. They are also the ones that prevent you from finding out what's really going on under the piles, people, or pounds. Because you're resisting the job so strongly, all you can think of is how far you are from the finish line, how much time and effort it's going to take to complete it, and how much of a pain it will be to even start.

You might think you can (and should) get it all done in one fell swoop. Maybe you believe that once you start, you can't stop until it's finished, or that there's a logical way to do it and if you can't do it that way, it can't be done at all. This all-or-nothing mindset is a default reaction of your fear. It's that part of you that feels completely overwhelmed. It focuses only on the before and after and struggles to see the process. However, it's the process—the small steps in between—that holds the secret to your success.

Breaking down your tasks and projects into smaller pieces increases your chances of getting started, which is the key to finishing anything. While Future You can easily get on board with how great it'll feel to have everything done, Present You needs consistent wins to stay motivated. With each small step you complete, you become more invested in finishing the whole task.

Engaging in this is simple. Instead of waiting until you have a free day to clean out your kitchen, get started right away by going through your utensil drawer. The next time you get dressed, look for one article of clothing you're willing to get rid of. When you're watching television at night, sort through a box from the garage. Take each big task one piece at a time.

---

## CASE STUDY: SAMANTHA

My client Samantha loves books. She's an avid reader who prefers paper over digital and buys new titles often. As such, she has accumulated hundreds, if not thousands of books. They live in her home office, but some spill into nearby rooms. She also has boxes in her garage that she plans to go through someday. She loves her books, so she's learned to live with the sheer volume of her collection, but it's so overwhelming. She feels stuck. How can she create order and keep her collection intact?

"Let's pare down the amount as a first step," I suggest. I ask her about her willingness to go through her books and look just for ones she's ready to part with.

"Oh, I couldn't," she says. "I can barely move in there, and I know I'll start reading or flipping through old books and lose sight of the task."

This is Samantha's main block. How can she get her books in order when they pull her in every time? Sometimes the obvious first step isn't always the right one, so we try a different approach.

"What if you start with boxing up all the books, regardless of whether you end up keeping them or not? Then put the boxes in another part of your house so that you can decide the best way to design or arrange your office. This way it can become a proper home for your collection."

"You mean just move them all out of there and not go through them?" she asks. "Wouldn't that be a waste of time? Doesn't it make more sense to go through them as I box them up?"

"Sure, in some cases that would make more sense, but so far it's proved to be less effective for you," I say. "The best approach is the one that works for you, so let's give this a go."

Samantha never would have thought of this option, because she tells herself she needs to leave all the books in that room until she goes through them. This is an unrealistic expectation for her because that's not how she operates. By giving her permission to customize her approach, we've upped her chances of doing something with the room—a room she'd like to be more inspiring and beautiful to support her writing.

"In fact, let's take a step back," I tell Samantha. "Find a picture online or from a magazine of a home office or library space that you would love to have. Let it be your inspiration for the room."

She browses on her phone for a few minutes and finds one she likes. It's a beautiful, light-filled room with floor-to-ceiling bookcases and a sliding ladder that moves back and forth. Best of all, it's open, organized, and a breath of fresh air. Just looking at it excites Samantha.

"I would be over the moon with that room! I could have all my books properly put away and still have space to breathe."

This became our new project: getting her office ready for those magnificent bookcases. In having that tangible vision—a vision that was believable and achievable—Samantha gained the resolve and enthusiasm she needed to box up her books.

Not long after she packed and moved them out, a designer came in to measure for new shelves.

"I can't believe this will be my new office and library," Samantha said, as she admired the picture she found. "And it's really happening!"

In just a few months after starting our work together, Samantha was back in her office with her boxes of books. She realized they all still brought her joy. They just needed to be honored with the proper storage. To someone else, this number of books might have been clutter, but to Samantha, they were treasures. By giving herself permission to take a different approach and reconfigure her expectations, Samantha was able to come up with a plan that was bigger and better than she'd ever imagined!

---

When you're realistic with your expectations, your resistance quiets down and you can get on board with the idea of sorting and clearing. By asking yourself to start with something small, you're more likely to see that true success is in the *action* rather than the *outcome*. Our stress is always caused by what we're not doing versus what we are. Because the key to finishing anything is starting it, you want to think about how you can make it easier to begin instead of focusing on the enormity of the job or how long it will take you to complete it.

## WHICH APPROACH WILL YOU TAKE?

Starting a project becomes easier when you determine whether it is better served by a section approach or a time approach. For example, let's say you want to go through all your dishes and pans. Labeling the task as "organize my kitchen" makes it way too broad, automatically turning it into a more difficult task. Instead, approach it cabinet-by-cabinet, one section at a time. When you have a finite section to work on, you have a shorter trip to the finish line, and the job feels more manageable. Complete one shelf and revel in your success, and you'll be less resistant when it comes to the next one.

The other way to handle a big job is in terms of time. Let's say you want to organize your garage. It's such a mess that you don't know where to begin. You can't even identify a good section to start with. In this scenario, you're best served by time goals. There are several methods of doing so, but my favorite is the Pomodoro technique.[1] This is a time management tool that can help you get started on just about anything. Here's how it works:

- Choose your task or project.
- Remove all distractions. Shut down your email, silence your phone, and close your door.
- When you're ready to begin, set a timer for 25 minutes. Work consistently until the timer rings.
- When the timer goes off, take a five-minute break away from the task. You've just completed one Pomodoro round (or POM round, as I call it. I like to think POM stands for "peace of mind").
- Repeat.
- After four POM rounds take a longer break, for 20 minutes or so.

The Pomodoro technique is great because it's simple and can be changed to suit you and your work style. Twenty minutes of work might be better for you, as could forty-five. Don't be so rigid that you don't get started (but don't over-think it either).

Once you get rolling, you may feel in the zone and not want to stop when the timer goes off. I say go for it! Keep going for as long as you'd like. However, at the first sign of dread or resistance, stop and step away for a bit. It's vital that you avoid creating a negative correlation with clutter clearing. You want your resistance to trust that you have her best interest at heart and that you won't ignore her pleas when she cries out. Acknowledging your resistance is a great way to quiet her down and give her the time she needs to recuperate.

Twenty-five minutes can fly by or it can feel like an eternity. It all depends on the job and how you feel in the moment. Try not to let your mood dictate your productivity. Follow through on your scheduled POM rounds no matter how you feel. When you want to throw in the towel, look at the timer and remind yourself how much longer you have. When the going gets tough, this should be you: "Nope, let's keep going. We have just sixteen minutes left."

There are still times when I loathe the idea of getting started on a round. When this happens, I implement a strategy I learned from a friend. I sit down for the POM round and set the timer. As the minutes tick by, I have one of only two choices: I can either work on the task at hand or I can sit there and do *absolutely nothing*. No going on social media, no checking email, no playing games on my phone. *Nothing.* When faced with these choices, diving into the task almost always wins because it's way harder to sit there for 25 minutes and do nothing.

In short: take a task one piece at a time. Setting realistic expectations of these super small steps is an almost-guaranteed way of getting started. Once you get started, you're good to go, go, go!

## BECOME FRIENDS WITH YOUR RESISTANCE

You've likely heard or read lots of advice about quieting your monkey mind, pushing through your resistance, and not entertaining the ego's influence. I actually recommend the exact opposite. The pushback you feel when you try to make progress is rooted in fear. The presence of your monkey mind, resistance, and ego are evidence that you're stepping out of your comfort zone. Everything in your comfort zone is familiar and safe, but it's also a place where no growth or change happens.

To help your resistance get on board and stay on board, let this be your mantra: "Underpromise and overdeliver." Nothing stops you in your tracks faster than thinking you need to do it all or do nothing. What's the benefit of getting nothing done, when you could get at least something done? Completing small steps makes it much more likely for you to finish the job, even if your fear says otherwise.

By not expecting yourself to dive into the deep end, you help that younger part of you trust the current you more. With each small step, she sees that you'll be right beside her, guiding her along the way. When she watches you take the lead, she'll be much more likely to step outside of her comfort zone. After all, she's not the one doing the adulting. You are. She needs you to do the heavy lifting as much as you need her playfulness and creative insight, so instead of trying to silence her, invite her to the party.

Furthermore, taking small steps gives you the courage you need to cross the line from the comfort zone into your stretch zone, where you can try new methods and motives. If things get too scary, you can always step back. Patience, compassion, and support are going to be far more successful than any kind of tough love. When you (the mature adult) and your younger self (your fear and resistance) team up, there will be no stopping you.

This doesn't mean you should indulge in your fear. You only need to acknowledge it, be aware of it, and hold space for it. That's usually all it needs to settle down. You can do this by simply naming your feelings as they come up:

"Oh, hello fear. I hear you."

"Hi, anxiety."

"I feel you, sadness."

It may feel a bit foolish, but this approach will teach you how to feel your feelings instead of analyzing them. Remember: feelings are not facts. They're guideposts.

## END THE DREAD

I once had a therapist tell me that I always have my "why" soldier at the ready. She said she noticed that whenever undesirable emotions flare up, I default to "why." "Why do I feel this way?" "Why did he do that?" "Why can't I catch a break?" I was always trying to think my feelings, but feelings are to be felt, not figured out or fixed.

It's human nature to want to run away from uncomfortable feelings, so we assign meaning to them, intellectualize them, or try and fix them—all of which is the same as telling our soul to shut up.

How often have you finally done something you've been putting off, only to be surprised at how much easier it was than you expected? You probably spent so much time and energy thinking about not wanting to do it or how long it would take, rather than actually getting it done.

I'm certainly guilty of this. (I think we all are.) I deplete my mental and physical energy on resisting the fact that I need or want to do something. When this becomes an issue, I think of this second mantra: "It takes longer to dread something than to do it."

I have a note posted by my computer reminding me of this because I can waste a lot of time thinking about when I'm going to do something or how to get out of having to do it at all. When that gets old, I tend to beat myself up for procrastinating. When I'm avoiding a project or distracting myself, I take a look at my mantra, go back to my trusty POM rounds, and get started with one 25-minute session. I quickly see how much better it feels to get the ball rolling.

## THE DIFFICULT DUO: PROCRASTINATION AND PERFECTIONISM

Realistic expectations are a critical aspect of creating space in your life. Breaking goals, projects, and tasks down into manageable bites not only ups your chances of success, but also allows you to experience the feelings of victory with each and every milestone. You needn't wait until everything is sorted to relish your win. You get that with each and every step.

While this may make sense logically, putting it into practice is something else. If you know that small steps are key, yet you still have trouble taking them, where do you turn? What could be stopping you? The culprits are likely one of two things (things that happen to be the best of friends): procrastination and perfectionism. Both cause us to protect ourselves, but more often than not, they feel like deep character flaws that are impossible to overcome.

You can thank unrealistic expectations for these two beauties. Procrastination convinces you that another day will be better. "I'll wait until I have a free weekend before I tackle that project." Then the weeks go by, and as you fill up your days, you leave little time to focus on what really matters.

Perfectionism keeps the bar too high, so you give yourself an easy out. "I can't complete this step, so why bother doing any of it?" This is a toxic way of thinking. Some progress is better than no progress, and a failed attempt is better than no attempt at all. And yet, the unrealistic expectations we have of ourselves keep both procrastination and perfectionism in our lives, serving as protectors of our self-doubt.

Consider the source of this self-doubt. It could be any one of the following: a fear of failure; a fear of success; a big step you have to overcome; someone else's high expectations of you; the possibility that, once finished, you might still not be happy; or any other source of anxiety in your life.

The best way to figure out what you're avoiding is by taking action. Start by looking at your next step and breaking it down. Keep breaking it down into smaller and smaller pieces until the step is so small that it takes more energy to avoid it than to complete it.

For example, let's say you've been procrastinating going through your teenage children's baby clothes. The task feels daunting and overwhelming. Do you donate them? Offer them to friends? What if you struggle to part with them at all?

These questions can easily stop you in your tracks if you let them. Instead, you can discover the answers to them by getting started. Maybe you begin with sorting just one bin into three piles: Keep, Donate, Friends. If that still feels too difficult, consider looking only for those items you are ready to part with. Any maybes stay for now. Still stuck? Grab your journal and write about how you feel at the idea of letting these items go.

When you stir the pot in this way, the true clutter rises to the surface. By digging in and getting started, it's almost as if you gently poke your resistance, waking it up so it can start chattering and tell you why it would rather you leave things alone. This is when you begin to uncover the message in the mess.

## PROCRASTINATION'S PAYOUT

If you still find yourself avoiding the task even after breaking it into pieces, it's time to dig deeper. There is something bigger you are scared of. Even if you know you'd be much happier, relieved, or excited with the project done, there is something more appealing about leaving it undone. Open your journal and ask yourself this question: "How am I benefitting from putting things off?" This question may sound ridiculous, but there must be a payout to procrastinating, otherwise you wouldn't be doing it. You might come up with answers like:

- If I complete this, people will expect more of me.
- I'm scared of the emotions this could stir up.
- I'm not smart enough to figure this out.
- What if I mess up and disappoint people?

It can be hard to face these thoughts. It's okay. Remember: the key is to start somewhere and to be kind to yourself as you do.

This is also a great example of a super small step you can take whenever you feel stuck. Super small steps are exactly that: super small and super easy. They don't need to be direct action related to the project you're procrastinating on. Sometimes the clutter we need to clear first is our resistance.

Play it out. Give it space to breathe. Humor it. That could be all it needs to get out of your way.

You can thank unrealistic expectations for all types of clutter. Keep the project out of reach, and the physical clutter remains. Start beating yourself up for not taking action, and your mental clutter piles up. Continue to live in pursuit of "someday," and your emotional clutter expands. However, all of this can be addressed by breaking things down. Just take it one piece at a time. As the saying goes, Rome wasn't built in a day.

Next, let's explore the stories you tell yourself that prevent you from clearing out.

### CHAPTER TAKEAWAYS

- Stubborn clutter is caused by one of or a combination of:
  a. Unrealistic expectations
  b. Limiting beliefs
  c. A need for boundaries

- The Pomodoro technique is a great tool to help you get started and stay focused on a task or project you've been avoiding.

- Super small steps will help you succeed every time.

- Befriend your resistance.

- Feelings are to be felt, not figured out or fixed.

## CHAPTER 3

# CORE CLUTTER CAUSE #2: LIMITING BELIEFS

The most significant thing you can do to eradicate the stubborn clutter in your life is to identify and dismantle old or limiting beliefs. They are, in most cases, the driving force behind it all. In fact, they're usually the source of your unrealistic expectations and the cause of your lack of boundaries—the other two core causes.

Limiting beliefs are powerful little buggers. They can prevent you from asking for help, booking your trip, going on that date, or ending a toxic relationship, all because of the stories you tell yourself.

Maybe you don't ask for help because you assume everyone is too busy to make time for you.

Perhaps you haven't planned that trip because you've been taught that traveling is a frivolous expense.

Maybe you've told yourself that you can't start dating because there's no way anyone could be attracted to you.

You might be staying in that unhealthy friendship because, well, that's just how it's always been.

It's this mindset, shaped by your beliefs, that eats up your time, keeps your hopes and dreams at bay, and has you tolerating unfulfilling relationships. And it's this mindset that creates the clutter you need to clear.

## WHEN ARE OUR BELIEFS FORMED?

When you're new in the world (typically between birth and age seven), you're constantly looking for guidance on how to navigate life. Courtesy of your underdeveloped brain, you operate from an egocentric place. You filter everything you do, see, and experience through the lens of "me."

How does this affect *me*?

What does this mean for *me*?

How do *I* survive in this scenario?

How do *I* react when something like that happens?

Because everything is about you, anything that happens around you becomes a part of your story. Because your brain's job is to seek answers, it's almost an automatic response for it to try to prove that an idea is true.

To stay safe in your community (the primary relationships in your life, including family, teachers, and friends), you make sense of any given situation by focusing on your role in it, even when it has nothing to do with you. You're not able to see that your mom's painful past is what's causing her to yell and scream. Instead, you tell yourself that you are the source of her troubles. As a result, you try to figure out how you can change your behavior to stop her from exploding. Thus, a belief is formed.

## BELIEFS START AS AN IDEA

When I was a young girl, my father would come home exhausted after working three jobs. He'd shuffle into the living room, where I often was playing, to watch TV. He'd plop into his favorite chair, kick off his shoes, and let out a big sigh. It was as if he'd melted into the cushions. But sometimes he wouldn't stay long.

After a few nights of him spending a short amount of time in the room with me, I wondered if I had anything to do with him leaving. After all, I was an emotional kid. I cried easily and fidgeted a lot, and being the youngest of seven children, he didn't have much patience left to deal with a little one.

I decided to test my theory. The next time he came in and sat down, I made a point to stay quiet and still. I said nothing and barely moved.

Dad stayed.

Coincidence? Maybe, but I wanted to be sure. I figured that if I wanted Dad to spend time with me, I could be seen, but I couldn't be heard, and my presence itself couldn't be distracting. I proved this over the next few nights by keeping myself quiet and still. And on every one of those nights, Dad sat in his comfy chair and stayed there. That was proof enough for me.

When your ideas are validated by words, actions, or experiences, they become beliefs. In his book *Awaken the Giant Within*, Tony Robbins likens it to a table. Your idea is the tabletop. The validation is the legs under the tabletop. Together, the legs and top form a belief. Without the legs to support the belief, it remains an idea.[2]

Dad staying when I remained still became the legs under my tabletop. And over the years, that table extended longer and longer, and my belief continued to grow stronger. The idea that Dad wouldn't leave as long as I stayed quiet evolved into a belief that affected me for years: people will love me as long as I didn't call attention to myself, take up too much space, or be needy.

While that may seem like a big leap, this is precisely how beliefs work. To my young brain, it made complete sense that I deserved love only on my father's terms—I even proved it! Surely, this was how all relationships were meant to work. At that point in my life, I had no frame of reference that told me otherwise.

## A SKEWED PERCEPTION

Your beliefs dictate how you see the world. Think of any pessimists you know. When presented with a scenario, they'll focus on the negative. The opposite is true for optimists. They'll focus on the positive. What you choose to look for is usually driven by an old story that was written in your life's instruction manual long ago. Because our brains need that constant validation to keep the belief alive, you unknowingly attract people and situations to support your beliefs. In fact, you'll seek them out too. After all, if you look hard enough for something—positive or negative—you'll find it. Whether big or small, positive or negative, beliefs are almost always a part of the picture.

---

## CASE STUDY: ABIGAIL

Abigail, a woman in my membership community, had accidentally collected numerous snow globes over the years. I say "accidentally" because she wasn't overly fond of them. What started with two she had bought as a souvenir soon became the default gift she received for every occasion. For every holiday, birthday, and celebration, someone would bring her a snow globe. She was sick of snow globes! And yet, she couldn't bring herself to donate them.

"I appreciate the kindness of these gifts, but I've never been much of a collector," said Abigail. "I'm more of a 'one or two that I love' kind of gal, but I still can't seem to let them go."

I shared my standing clutter rule of thumb with her: "If you don't love it, need it, or use it, it's clutter. Do your snow globes fit into any of those categories? Do you love them, need them, or use them?"

"I do love them," she said. "Well, I love the thought behind the gift, I guess. Not the actual items. I mean, some are pretty, but I'd be all right without them."

"Okay, great! Then off they go!"

"Oh, I couldn't," Abigail said. "I'd feel guilty donating them."

I knew that feeling. "I can appreciate that. So would you say you're keeping them more out of guilt than joy?"

"I guess so, yes," Abigail said.

"Then the snow globes are only a small portion of the clutter you're dealing with. There's some emotional clutter that needs your attention too—and likely before the snow globes."

I asked Abigail to tell me more about the guilt she felt when she considered donating these gifts.

"It was so kind of people to give them to me. I don't want to appear ungrateful."

"What would happen if someone thought that of you?"

"It wouldn't feel very good! And it could damage our relationship."

"Have you had that happen in the past?" I asked.

"No, but no one likes a thankless person. Who wants to be around someone like that?"

As we continued to dig, more and more of Abigail's beliefs were rising to the surface. We learned that it's not acceptable if someone else considers you ungrateful. What's more, people don't like ungrateful individuals. They often end up alone and forgotten. If all of that were true, I wouldn't get rid of the snow globes either!

Together, Abigail and I considered the possible outcomes of her donating the snow globes. Maybe the gift giver would be relieved to learn Abigail didn't keep something because she felt she had to. Maybe Abigail would survive feeling guilty and fill the new space with things or experiences she loves. A lot of good things could come of it, we decided. But she still needed convincing.

"As an overgiver myself, Abigail, I've learned to see guilt as a sign that I'm taking good care of my needs. It's also good to consider—since you've been making your decision from a place of obligation—where else in your life do you tend to do things for that same reason?"

We ended our coaching session with an action plan for Abigail: donate three snow globes and spend time journaling about guilt and obligation, asking herself questions like "What do these things mean to me?" and "How are they holding me back from achieving my dreams?" We'd see how she felt afterward.

During our call the next week, Abigail was both excited and angry.

"Guess what?" she said. "I donated ten globes last week! It felt a bit naughty, but I was ultimately relieved."

"Damn, Abigail! That's fantastic!"

"And now I'm kind of pissed," she said.

*Uh-oh. Was she having regrets? Did I push her too far?*

"I've wasted so much of my life doing what I think others want me to do," she said. "When is it my turn?"

"It's always been your turn," I told her.

"I realize that now, which is why I'm mad. What have I been waiting for? Someone to give me permission?"

"Well, kind of, yes. And that 'someone' is you. And you've now given yourself permission. Thus begins an exciting new chapter of your life, Abigail!"

The phone went quiet for a moment. I heard a loud exhale, and even through the distance between us, I felt her energy shift from regret to potential.

"You've done your absolute best up until this point," I said. "You couldn't have made this move any sooner. You weren't ready. But you are now. So well done. Onward and upward!"

"Onward and upward, indeed," Abigail said quietly.

How about that? Abigail's world opened up, ripe with new possibilities and opportunities for growth. All because she donated some snow globes, it seems. But by now you know that it's never just about the stuff.

Abigail's beliefs about being ungrateful not only caused her to keep things she no longer loved (physical clutter), but also to struggle with her feelings about it (emotional clutter). She was tortured by her inner critic, who was telling her what she should and shouldn't be doing (mental clutter), and even found herself feeling resentful toward friends she feared would judge her (relationship clutter).

This is how powerful limiting beliefs are—they warp your perspective into what your brain thinks is true. But you can challenge your old beliefs and revise them to fit who you are and what you want to accomplish today.

---

Similar to Abigail, the belief that I shouldn't be needy has been at the root of my relationship clutter, health clutter, calendar clutter, and more, all throughout my life. When I operate from this mindset, I tend to attract a lot of needy people because, on the outside, I appear to have it all together. Combine that with my other belief that I have to be important to be valued, and you can likely imagine where I land on my priority list (hint: it's not at the top).

When I behave from these limiting beliefs, I teach others that I'm happy to give, even at the expense of my own needs. People tell me how great I am at finding solutions, scoring deals, doing internet research—you name it. These accolades only validate my beliefs more, making them even stronger. Since they were encoded in my brain as a child, it's been hard to let go of them.

Because you're young when you write these instructions, they don't often stay relevant as you grow into an adult. They don't just disappear, though. They linger, and if they linger too long and too loudly, they can have an adverse effect on you (like Abigail's need to keep her snow globes). You must realize when they're driving your decisions and behavior and intentionally work on dismantling them. I started to do this for myself while I was in college.

The summer after my freshman year, I worked as an orientation leader with a group of my fellow students. Ten of us lived together in the dorm for six weeks as we participated in team building exercises and learned how to best represent the school for the incoming freshmen. During this process, I quickly became friends with another orientation leader named Melissa.

She was someone I came to trust in a way I never had before. While I kept on my shield that said "no needs here" for a while, I also saw this as an opportunity to have a different kind of friendship than I was used to. Maybe I could rely on someone else for a change, if only a little. Despite my old belief waving the warning flag, I began to slowly drop my protective wall. I would test the waters by sharing a tiny bit of vulnerability with her, and when I saw her lean in instead of turn away, I'd share more.

My friendship with Melissa challenged my belief that people wouldn't stick around if I had needs. It felt scary, but it was exciting! I was terrified that she'd eventually tire of my "weakness," but she proved me wrong again and again. She became the first person I could be my full, true self with, and it became a type of friendship I didn't know could exist.

This changed the way I behaved in my relationships with both family and friends. I softened a bit and let more people in. I was less afraid to be myself. As a result, other friendships deepened and, most importantly, the relationship I had with myself became more authentic. The journey didn't come without speed bumps, however.

Fast forward several years when I became good friends with a woman named Amy. We had a lot of the same interests, and we both liked having philosophical and existential conversations. Amy and I would go hiking, attend workshops, and play soccer together. We seemed to be on the same wavelength. I felt like she "got" me. We'd talk about how difficult it could be to find friends as an adult, especially friends who were as easily bored with small talk as we were. I'd often joke with her that I was going to start a website, Peoplewhogetit.com, as a friendship-dating site of sorts.

I let down my wall with Amy. We each shared personal things, and our friendship grew as a result. I guess I was getting better at attracting my people!

One Sunday afternoon, Amy and I planned to spend some time together. We were going to go for a nature walk and catch up. It wasn't anything high-pressure.

The time we'd scheduled for came and went. I wasn't terribly concerned, as she had a habit of running late.

Then an hour went by. Then another. I tried calling and texting her, leaving messages and hearing nothing back. I started to feel worried. *Was she in an accident? Was she okay?* I kept trying to call her and leaving messages but got no response.

I couldn't think of anyone else to contact to see if she was okay, so I spent the afternoon switching between concern and anger. Would she really blow me off? We'd just talked about this plan on Friday!

Later that night, I hopped onto Facebook to see what my friends were up to and I noticed that Amy had "liked" a post someone made—a post that was only two hours old. She was alive. She was safe! And I was mad. She couldn't even call me to cancel. I'd waited for her all day. The least she could do was give me a reason why.

I called her the next day. No answer. I waited a few days and called again. Nothing. I tried a week later. Silence.

At that point I gave up. I had no idea what I'd done to upset her, but there was nothing more I could do. Then my old belief kicked in the door, waving its arms and screaming.

"See? This is what happens when you share too much of yourself. You're too needy, too emotional. You never should have leaned on her for support."

This sent me down a shame spiral for quite some time. I pulled back from other friends, increased my giving game, and beat myself up for being so vulnerable. My old behavior was back. It was time for me to reach into my emotional and spiritual toolbox and pull out the opposite, empowering belief I created during my friendship with Melissa: "The more I share of myself, the deeper my relationships become."

I wasn't about to let this experience with Amy set me back. I had come too far—not only in terms of personal growth, but because I truly considered us friends. In honor of that fact, I began re-engaging with friends and sharing (selectively) with people I trusted.

As it turns out, Amy disappeared because of a recurring personal issue in her life that I had supported her through before. She was embarrassed for me to see it happening again, so she avoided me, thinking I'd judge her and be annoyed. It seems that one of her limiting beliefs smacked up against mine, though neither of us knew it at the time. We talked it out, openly and honestly, and were able to move past it.

## HOW TO IDENTIFY YOUR BELIEFS

Because beliefs are such a tightly woven part of who you are, it can be difficult to recognize when they're a driving force in your life. Taking a stroll down memory lane and thinking about times when you were a child is a great way to discover any belief that keeps getting in your way. You can also pay attention to any generalizing language you use, such as:

- I can never catch a break.
- Why does it always have to be so hard?
- I'll never be able to afford that.
- It's best if I keep my opinion to myself.

These broad statements, which are often said in frustration, construct the lens through which you see life. The more you use them, the more you'll approach situations anticipating getting the short end of the stick, looking for things to be hard, and feeling like you have to swallow your voice. Your brain will go on autopilot to validate these ideas and slant the way you interpret your experiences. If you believe you'll never be able to succeed, you're going to live your life proving yourself right.

Try this exercise to discover even more disruptive thinking:

- **Make a list of any general belief you hold.** Think about topics such as religion, politics, family, success, and wealth. Make sure they're beliefs you feel strongly about and that impact how you live your life.

- **Evaluate each belief.** Which of your listed beliefs make you feel good? Which ones make you feel crappy? This will be your first clue. The ones that make you feel hopeless, powerless, or as if they hold you down are likely sources of clutter. As such, you'll find them in any area of your life where you're stuck or overwhelmed. For example, if you believe money struggles are just your lot in life, you likely have financial clutter, whether that is debt, past tax returns that haven't been filed, or a penchant for impulse shopping.

  Look for areas where every time you take a step forward, you end up taking two steps back. You can also look for things you've been talking about forever but have never gotten around to doing. There's likely a belief causing you to put it off.

- **Open your journal and conduct an interview with yourself.** Pose a question and then let it flow. No censoring. No editing. No erasing. Just free-write. It might go something like this:

  "What is stopping me from starting that blog?"

  "I don't even know how to do it. Do I need a website? Does it cost anything? What would I even write about? Would anyone read it? How is it different than keeping a journal? What if nobody cares? Who am I to say I'm an expert?

You have to be pretty self-centered to write a blog. And do I even want to deal with the online comments?"

- **List the evidence for each belief.** Once you've finished, take a look at your work. Is there any evidence of beliefs in what you wrote in your journal? If so, write them down. In the blog example above, there is plenty of validation:

  - I have nothing important to say.

  - Who do I think I am? I'm no expert!

  - If you write a blog, you're a self-absorbed narcissist.

  - If I put myself out there, people will be hurtful and mean.

  It's these stories that fuel your perfectionism and procrastination. Maybe you tell yourself that you never finish what you start, or that you're not smart enough to own a business. You might believe that, if you can't get it all done, then you shouldn't bother starting. Perhaps you're afraid of sounding silly in an otherwise professional line of work.

- **Come up with an opposite, empowering belief for each limiting one you identified.** Take a few minutes and come up with an opposite belief to counteract any you listed. Working on the previous list, here are some examples:

  - If what I have to say is important to me, that's enough.

  - I'm an expert on myself, and no one can be me better than I can.

- Bloggers are generous creators eager to connect.

- What other people think of me is none of my business.

How differently would life be if you operated from these new beliefs? Does that idea make you feel excited? Scared? A combination of the two (always a good sign in my book!)?

It's easy to use a limiting belief as an excuse to not take action, especially when you don't know you're doing it. Sometimes these stories are hidden pretty deep behind your procrastination. Here's a cool trick to try whenever you're putting something off: think about what comes after the step you're dragging your feet on. Is the move after the next particularly intimidating? Could the payout to procrastinating be that you can avoid the step after the next?

---

## CASE STUDY: MATTHEW

A member of one of my coaching groups, Matthew, needed to find a job. However, he kept putting it off, and didn't seem to have a reason why. He would talk about what a mess his desk was, or how his resume was outdated. How could he possibly apply for an open position with such glaring obstacles in his way?

"What if updating your resume is the step you need to take to get your desk in order?" I asked him. "Maybe it's not the other way around?"

I suggested that he work at his dining room table for now to expedite the application process. He agreed and reluctantly promised to update his resume by the next time our group met.

When Matthew's turn in the coaching hot seat came, he jumped right in. "I tried to do my resume, but it needs a lot more work than I thought. I got overwhelmed and put it aside. I did get some piles cleared from my desk, though."

Using the trick above, I asked Matthew how he'd feel if, after sending out some resumes, he was called in to interview.

"They're certainly not my strong suit. In fact, they kind of terrify me. I never know what to say. The last time I interviewed, I froze and answered questions with 'I don't know,' and 'Yeah, I guess.'"

Now we were getting somewhere. Matthew was keeping his desk messy and his resume outdated so he wouldn't have to go on an interview, which freaked him out. He thought that the disorganized desk was his biggest roadblock when it came to job hunting. In truth, it was his belief that he sucked at interviewing.

The stuff on Matthew's desk was symptomatic clutter. The core clutter was the limiting belief and the resulting lack of confidence when it came to being interviewed. To begin the real cleanup, I had him research tips on successful interviewing and do some practice rounds with someone he trusted. The more comfortable Matthew became with interviewing, the easier it would become to clear his desk, update his resume, and apply for jobs.

---

## OLD BELIEFS HOLD YOU DOWN

When you're behaving at the direction of an old belief, you're much less likely to take risks, even calculated ones. Your fear is firmly planted in this outdated way of thinking because it's so familiar. It's been validated for years, after all!

Staying in your comfort zone may be comfortable, but that's where your old life lives. To make the changes you've been hungry for, you need to step outside of it.

This is when it's time to rewrite your life's instruction manual by challenging the beliefs that are blocking your path. You, too, can upgrade your operating system and live more in a way that is aligned with who you are today. Thank your old beliefs for their service (they were needed at one point, otherwise you wouldn't have created them) and let them know you'll take it from here.

In the chapters to come, we'll explore specific clutter hotspots that have limiting beliefs rumbling underneath so you can learn how to clear them from this powerful, core place.

## CHAPTER TAKEAWAYS

- Limiting beliefs are part of an outdated instruction manual you created for your life long ago. While they served you well in the past, you have now outgrown them. They prompt you to behave or think in a certain way that keeps you playing by old rules and prevent you from leveling up your life.

- Pay attention to the stories you tell yourself about your family and friends, your hopes and dreams, and any situations around you. They hold clues to your limiting beliefs.

- Where have you felt stuck for a long time, where you take one step forward and two steps back? There's likely a belief in play here.

- When you can't seem to make any progress, open your journal and ask yourself the following question: "What am I really afraid of?" Let your soul speak through your pen. No censoring. No editing.

## CHAPTER 4

# CORE CLUTTER CAUSE #3: A LACK OF BOUNDARIES

B oundaries are complicated. On one hand, they are the second biggest cause of clutter. On the other, they are an effective tool for living your best life. They set the standard for how you want to be treated—not only by others, but by yourself as well. When you set boundaries, your relationships flourish, your health improves, your home is more organized, and your professional success skyrockets. Yes, they are that powerful!

Conversely, a lack of boundaries can cause every type of clutter. Whether you're tolerating someone's inappropriate behavior, using piles of stuff in your home as an excuse not to host the holidays, or agreeing to chip in for something you can't afford, your inability (or unwillingness) to set boundaries affects relationships of all kinds. Not only that, it can affect your physical and mental health as well. Without healthy boundaries, you may face weight gain, depression, struggles with self-worth, and the notion of living for someday rather than today.

It can be tricky to see how desperately you need boundaries because you might be used to tolerating the poor behavior of others. You may not realize there's another option. We often confuse difficult choices with no choice at all, and since speaking up can be especially difficult at times, the idea simply may not come to mind.

You also may hesitate to draw a line in the sand if old beliefs are instructing you otherwise. This is where the core causes of clutter can pile up. Your outdated thinking might cause you to forgo boundaries in favor of what you believe to be true. For example, maybe you think that by limiting the time you're available to your draining friend, you run the risk of losing her altogether. Or you believe asking for help is a sign of weakness, so you take everything on your shoulders. When you neglect setting boundaries, you impact much more than a particular scenario or relationship.

---

## CASE STUDY: EMMA

My client Emma works as a graphic designer at an advertising agency. She gets to use her creativity to help clients' businesses and brands shine, and she performs her duties both collaboratively and independently. She loves her job. Mostly. It would be perfect if it wasn't for Sean. Sean is Emma's direct supervisor. He often speaks to her in a condescending tone and makes it obvious that he favors her fellow designer, Brian. Since Emma is one of only two women at the agency, she feels like she's infiltrating the boys' club.

"He'll dismiss my ideas in our brainstorming meetings, calling them 'silly' or 'juvenile,'" Emma says. "It feels humiliating and makes me not want to speak up anymore."

"Is it that he doesn't like your ideas that makes you feel bad, or how he delivers his feedback?" I ask.

"Both, but more so how he shoots them down so harshly."

"Have you considered talking to him about it?"

"For maybe a second," Emma says, "but then I don't bother. He won't listen to me anyway."

"What makes you think that?" I ask.

"I can't expect him to coddle me, not that I want him to. But because I'm a woman, he'll probably think I'm whining or being too sensitive."

"Has anyone in the past ever called you a whiner or told you that you're too sensitive?"

"Other than society as a whole?" She laughs half-heartedly. "Sure, I grew up with all brothers. If I scraped myself up or had my feelings hurt, the standard response was 'Oh, you're fine.' But I wasn't always fine."

After that revelation, the picture came into focus. To survive her male-dominated family dynamic, Emma learned to suck it up when things weren't okay. There was no room for the discussion or expression of feelings. It's no wonder she never planned on talking with Sean. She had never set boundaries for herself. Instead, she lived on the edge of the boundaries her family had created.

Emma and I work on this for several months. Our goal is to have her rewrite her old beliefs and set healthy boundaries of her own—boundaries that will help her own her power when someone pushes her. Emma challenges herself to ask safe friends for help more often. In doing so, she strengthens her courage muscles, not only with her own might, but with the support of her loved ones. In time, we create a script for her to use when she speaks to Sean.

Emma's still a bit shaky, but she schedules a meeting with him. I make sure to provide her some sandwich support: speaking with her right before the meeting to remind her to be succinct, clear, and direct, and then again right after to celebrate her courage regardless of how the meeting goes. She's terrified before going into the meeting, but when she calls me after, she sounds fired up!

"I still feel a bit jittery, but I feel powerful too! Sean was defensive at first but then softened as I explained my side. By the end he seemed to look at me with more respect," Emma says.

"That's fantastic! I'm so proud of you," I say. "And even if he had stayed defensive, it would have been a win. Remember: success is in the action, not the outcome. Well done."

Emma's frustration with her supervisor was taking a toll on a job she loved. By being willing to stand up for herself and let him know his behavior is not acceptable with her, she now gets to go to work without the weight on her chest she had been feeling for years.

## WHERE DO YOU NEED A BOUNDARY?

Your body and your gut are great barometers to help determine where you need to set boundaries. Pay attention to when you feel wiped out, disrespected, ignored, or taken advantage of by someone.

If you spend your time on things or with people who are not supportive of the life you want to be living, you need a boundary.

When you say yes when you want to say no, you need a boundary.

Remember this: Boundaries are not about eliminating people from your life. In fact, it's just the opposite. You create boundaries when you care about someone enough to salvage and strengthen your relationship with them and clear any clutter that is in the way. Without them, you sacrifice your time, your needs, and your dreams.

## THE BOUNDARY BREAKERS

When evaluating the relationships in your life, consider the following types of people:

1. **The Commiserator:** This person is the embodiment of the phrase "misery loves company." They connect with others through bitching and complaining. They are either incapable or unwilling to share in someone's joy and will usually find the negative in any news they receive. When spending time with the Commiserator, you might find yourself eating, drinking, yawning, or tuning out of the conversation more than you typically would. When you return home, you're exhausted and annoyed, and the thought of seeing them again fills you with dread.

2. **The Dumper:** This person reaches out to vent all their woes onto you. Despite this, they aren't interested in receiving advice or suggestions, and rarely ask how you're doing. If they do, they're quick to one-up your struggle with one of their own or rain on your parade with snide comments like "Must be nice." Similar to time spent with the Commiserator, you might find yourself tuning out of the conversation and leave feeling annoyed at the Dumper's unwillingness to take action to improve their life. You might start avoiding their calls and messages, knowing that they're only looking for a sounding board. It being you on the other end holds no significance. They simply choose the person who will let them dump. They leave the conversation feeling lighter and better—for a short period of time—and you leave feeling weighed down and wiped out.

3. **The Victim:** This person believes everything that happens in their life has been done *to* them. They've been dealt a bad hand and always get a raw deal. They sit back and wait for a break to come their way, which, of course, never comes. This only deepens their "poor me" attitude. If you dare to suggest any steps to improve their situation, they'll tell you all the reasons they won't work. Many of their responses start with, "Yeah, but . . ." They'd much rather stay stuck than make the smallest change, and no matter how hard you try, you'll likely always want more for them than they want for themselves.

4. **The Damsel in Distress:** This person is forever seeking a rescue. They desperately want someone or something to fix whatever they deem broken in their life. They aren't interested in doing the heavy lifting, but they kid themselves into thinking that the next course, book, or seminar will contain the magic solution to their long-term struggle. They likely have good intentions and want to improve their life, but they struggle to make it happen. You tire of cheering them on as they share the latest diet, productivity hack, or guru message that is finally going to change their life, if only because you know they'll be on to something else next week.

Does any of the above describe someone you know? Perhaps a friend, family member, boss, spouse, or neighbor? Maybe even you? There's no shame here!

I've been the Damsel in Distress, and as hard as that is to admit, recognizing it allowed me to see my actions from a bigger perspective. From there, I could explore the deeper reasons as to why I felt incapable or resistant to doing the work myself. All of our self-sabotaging measures are opportunities for growth.

Just like you and me, the people described above are doing the best they can. However, they can be major energy vampires who will deplete you and prevent you from focusing on what really matters: your happiness. Neglect to set boundaries with any of these people and you'll quickly become one of them.

## REPAIR OR REPLACE?

Now that you've identified where you could use a boundary or two, how do you go about it?

When you think about establishing or setting a boundary, do you envision a scary, confrontational conversation? Do you see yourself puffing out your chest and standing up to the bully? This is often what most of my clients imagine when we broach the subject. They're always surprised to learn that that is actually quite uncommon.

The first step when considering what to do with a strained relationship is to determine if it's even worth a boundary. I call this "Repair or Replace." In most cases, it'll be a repair. That said, it's good to check in and make sure, so don't gloss over this part! First, ask yourself the following questions, being as honest as possible (after all, this is for your eyes only!):

- How important is this person to you?
- Is the need for boundaries the only or main issue in the relationship?
- If the relationship could be healthy and balanced, would you be excited to have this person in your life?

- How long have you been tolerating this person's behavior?

- Have you set boundaries in the past that didn't stick?

- Is it possible to remove this person from your life, or are they someone you'll see again and again?

Answering these questions will help you do a health check of the relationship and determine if it's salvageable. When looking at your responses, do they describe the type of relationship you want? If not, what might be stopping you from saying good-bye to this person? You may just uncover some limiting beliefs that are inviting you to challenge them.

Here are some examples:

**Belief:** I should stay friends with Meghan because I've known her for a long time.

**Challenge:** What if ending this unfulfilling friendship makes room for more soul family friendships for both me and Meghan?

**Belief:** Staying in my marriage is best for our kids.

**Challenge:** What if it's best for our kids for me to leave the toxic relationship?

**Belief:** I need to keep my brother in my life despite his violent outbursts, because he's family.

**Challenge:** What if I focused my energy on the family—biological and chosen—who lifts me up instead of beats me down?

It can be tough to challenge your beliefs. It can be even tougher to consider removing someone from your life, especially if they've been in it for a long time. If you choose to keep them around, be sure you're doing it for reasons that are aligned with who you are today—not who you used to be or who you could be.

Process your emotions around the relationship. Allow yourself to feel whatever comes up for you. Hold space for these emotions by journaling or meditating. Talk it through with a trusted family member or friend who can help you find your own way.

## PREPARE TO REPLACE

If you have decided it's time to let someone go, have a plan. Will you simply never talk to them again? Will you tell them you no longer have time to devote to the relationship? Do you want to let them know why you're opting out? Whatever approach is best for you is the one to go with. If you choose to talk to them about it, have support ready, whether it's a trusted friend, family member, or coach who you can talk to right before and after.

## THE PROCESS OF REPAIRING

For the relationships you've determined worthy of repair (yes, *worthy*), it's time to restructure the dynamic between you using the powerful tool of boundaries. Depending on who you're dealing with and the type of relationship you have with them, there are several approaches you can take:

- **Behavioral:** A behavioral boundary is when you show the person, through your actions, what is acceptable and what isn't. For example, if a coworker is gossiping about someone, you convey your feelings by not contributing to the conversation or by walking out of the room.

This is also a great way to handle someone who calls, texts, or messages you too much. Take more time to respond to teach them how often you prefer to connect and to let them know you are not at their beck and call. Instead of texting right back, wait an hour. Instead of calling them immediately, wait until the morning. Take your time. Changes in your behavior send a silent message to the offender that you're not interested in communicating as often. If this works, and you find the person adjusting their behavior with you, you're done! If more is needed, see below.

- **Direct:** A direct boundary is when you clearly communicate what you will and will not allow in a relationship. Some examples are "I don't accept phone calls after 8 P.M.," "Please don't tell racist jokes in my company," or "It's not okay to make comments about my body or weight." By sending a direct message, you are communicating your needs effectively and honestly. Sometimes, however, that still may not be enough. This is when you step things up by being firm.

- **Firm:** A firm boundary is when you strongly course-correct someone's behavior toward or around you. This is a necessary follow-up when a direct boundary is ignored. It needn't be confrontational, but it does need to be strong, and you need to hold your ground. For example, you might say something like, "I've asked you several times to not tell racist jokes in my company. If you continue to do it, I'll no longer be able to spend time with you." By being firm with the person in question, you are leaving them no choice but to respect your boundary or face the consequences. Making the consequences clear is paramount to your success, as is following through with them.

Once you've set a boundary, then the real work begins. For the guideline to stick, you must follow it up with action. For example, if you tell your sister that you don't accept phone calls after 8 P.M. but answer her at 8:30 P.M., you've essentially told her to disregard what you said.

Setting and then ignoring your own boundaries is one of the top two reasons many boundaries fail. Each time you break your own boundaries, you teach others to do the same. To have healthy, balanced relationships where you feel respected, heard, and significant, it's critical that you honor yourself enough to tolerate nothing less.

The other main reason a boundary fails is when you say too much. When teaching someone how to treat you or declining a request or invitation, there are two important things to remember when choosing your words: keep it short, sweet, and to the point; do not overexplain. The more concise, the better. Saying something like, "Sorry I can't make the party. I hope you have a great time," is much more effective than, "Sorry I can't make the party, but I have company coming into town next weekend, and I have a lot of preparations I need to make before they get here."

The second response invites debate. By explaining your answer, you leave room for the other person to offer solutions. They might respond with, "Can't you get that stuff done before the party so you can come?"

Similarly, when letting someone know their treatment of you is not okay, the same rules apply. Saying "Please don't speak to me that way" is more powerful than saying

"Please don't speak to me that way because it embarrasses me and hurts my feelings." Any time you offer too much, you weaken your position and appear shaky in your stance. The person may respond with something like, "Oh, you're just too sensitive," giving themselves permission to continue behaving the way they have been and making the problem *you* instead of *them*. You also convey that you need the other person to agree with your boundary for it to matter. This is obviously not the case. Your boundary matters to you, and that's what's important.

Even when you've prepared yourself emotionally and logistically for this conversation, you may find yourself putting it off. Maybe tolerating their behavior is easier than asking them to stop. Maybe saying yes all the time feels safer than facing the consequences you've made up in your head. It's likely that, as with any clutter, there's a payoff to letting it remain. Something about keeping the relationship as is benefits you in a way that feels more comfortable than rocking the boat. The pain and aggravation of the clutter is not yet greater than the fear of change.

When this payoff pulls you back, multiple core causes of clutter have joined forces to keep you stuck. What's likely stopping you from setting your boundaries is an old belief telling you that it's not okay to speak up or make your needs known. Maybe you don't want to risk making someone mad, or you fear appearing selfish or not being liked. When you hesitate to make your needs a priority, listen for the story you're telling yourself. It's in there that you'll discover the real clutter.

## WHAT DOES A HEALTHY BOUNDARY LOOK LIKE?

As I shared with you before, I can be an overgiver. Sure, I like to help people. I always have. However, I don't always do it from an altruistic place. My belief that I have to be valuable to be loved can cause me to swoop in and try to be a hero in situations that are none of my concern. As a result, my boundaries get shaky or disappear altogether.

My beliefs become the driving force behind my inability to set a boundary. Sometimes they prevent me from seeing that I even need one, because I naturally expect myself to do too much for others, often at the expense of my own needs. When this happens, I get frustrated by any requests that come my way. I give, give, give and then blow. Therefore, I have to be aware of whether I'm helping out of kindness or if I'm doing it in hopes of earning love and appreciation.

Stretching myself so thin leaves me wiped out with no energy for tidying or cleaning, so physical clutter piles up around me. I beat myself up for not tending to the mess I've made, adding mental clutter to the mix. My empty emotional tank often drives me to comfort food, adding to my weight clutter. My anger over loved ones not meeting expectations they don't even know I've set for them creates a cluttered mess in our relationships.

Can you believe how intricate clutter is?

This is no one's fault but my own. I've given people this expectation of myself. I've taught them how to be in a relationship with me for years, so it's not fair of me to get aggravated when they behave the way I've trained them. Instead, I need to change the way I behave with them.

Let's imagine a situation with healthy boundaries in place. A friend of mine casually mentions being a bit nervous about an upcoming doctor's appointment. Instead of offering to go with her (something I would typically do without hesitation), I listen to her empathetically as she shares her feelings. I might ask her when it is and park that in the back of my mind to later revisit the option of going with her. Later that day, I check my calendar to see if I am available to go with her. If I'm not, then the situation is put to bed. There's nothing more to do here.

It turns out I don't have a time conflict at the time of her appointment, but I still want to consider my needs before offering. Being available for someone isn't just about having the time to spare. It's important to make sure you're emotionally and energetically available. *Do I feel like I have the capacity to emotionally support someone right now? Do I have the energy to spare? Will I regret going? What is my motivation behind offering?*

As I sit with the idea some more, I feel tension in my body. Things have been hectic lately, and that free afternoon feels like such a gift. It also feels indulgent. *Am I worth claiming it as my own? Is it okay to rest on the couch and read instead of going to the doctor with my friend?* My belief tells me no, but my body says, "Oh yes!" With that, I choose to not go with her, and instead let her know that I'm around if she wants to talk before or after.

The day of the appointment arrives. As I enjoy my downtime, I wrestle with guilt over not going but also feel proud for making myself a priority. When my friend calls after her appointment, I am able to be fully present with her, without resentment or feelings of regret. I'm careful to not apologize over and over or make it a big deal that I didn't go with her— after all, it was never really about me, was it? As a result, our friendship remains healthy and strong, and my belief about having to earn love is dismantled some more.

On the surface, setting boundaries can sound scary, and without thoughtful approaches, they can be difficult and uncomfortable. Considering all of these aspects is how you stop teaching others that you'll drop everything for them all the time. In doing so, you prevent yourself from becoming frustrated when they expect it of you. Pausing before answering is a great way to avoid having to place a corrective boundary in the future, and you will be well-prepared to set them firmly and graciously.

Now that we've explored the three core causes of clutter, let's have a look at how they play out in some of the most common types of clutter. As you read the next several chapters and think about the obstacles you have in the featured areas, keep these three causes in mind to help you identify the message in your mess.

## CHAPTER TAKEAWAYS

- Boundaries are not always about eliminating people from your life.

- When you allow others to infiltrate your energetic space, you send a message to yourself and to others that your needs don't matter.

- By overgiving to others, you leave no time, energy, or bandwidth for yourself and your life. Your soul will throw a temper tantrum and get your attention through clutter—physical, emotional, and mental.

- Healthy boundaries foster fulfilling and inspiring relationships.

- Practice disappointing one person a day for two weeks and see what you learn about yourself.

## CHAPTER 5

# TAKE YOUR POWER BACK FROM PAPERWORK

Despite us living in an advanced digital age, the amount of paperwork that continues to accumulate in our homes is astounding. Whether it's catalogs and junk mail or printed blog posts and insurance policies, it can feel impossible to keep up with.

As one of the most common forms of clutter, paperwork takes over your desk, dining room table, counters, and shelves, and piles up so quickly it can feel like it's always two (or ten!) steps ahead of you. For being a pile of thin sheets, you wouldn't think it could be so powerful, but it is.

Because the papers in the piles are often bills, credit card statements, insurance policies, to-do lists, legal documents, tax returns, and forms to be signed, they represent some pretty grown-up stuff. Paperwork clutter can say a lot about what's working in your life and what's not.

When left disorganized, these stacks can suffocate your financial health, reinforce negative money beliefs, chip away at your confidence, and stop you from playing bigger in the world. In dealing with this category of clutter, you can learn about your money mindset, fear of success, relationship blocks, and disbelief that you have what it takes. As such, dealing with them can be intimidating. That intimidation can trigger fear and cause you to regress to your younger self.

When this little one is running the show, it's difficult to tackle such heavy clutter. When it piles up and gets away from you, it can make you feel small, incapable, and less than. This isn't the way you want to be around your finances and personal and professional success. You want to feel capable and empowered.

While you might think you're neglecting paperwork clutter because you're lazy, disorganized, or incapable of handling it, I can guarantee there's more to it.

I had a small pile of paperwork on my desk. It wasn't taking up much space at all. Energetically, however, it felt like it was consuming the room. It was always there, almost like it was watching me. Most of the papers were things I needed to follow up on quickly, but I found myself procrastinating for months. I later learned I was doing so because two of the papers had more to them than I realized.

One was a note on a brief brainstorming session where I captured some business ideas. Another was a quote I'd received from my vet to have my cat's teeth cleaned.

Every now and then I'd pick up these documents, flip through them, tap them on the desk to tidy them up, and put them back down. Have you ever done the Clutter Shuffle—touching something and moving it to feel like you've somehow made progress on it?

Why was I dragging my feet on this? I sure was sick of seeing these papers on my desk, but clearly not sick enough to do anything about them. Eventually I asked myself, *What would I tell a client?*

Ah yes. I'd tell them to do a POM round. I would set a timer for 25 minutes and focus exclusively on the task at hand. And this was a perfect time to use that tool.

In my first 25-minute round, I handled the easy stuff. I made a phone call to fix an incorrect bill and another to ask my health insurance company about a mystery notice. I finished both before the timer even went off! I remembered that it really does take longer to dread something than to do it. The daunting papers remained—my brainstorm of business ideas and the quote to have my cat's teeth cleaned. I found myself looking for distractions.

*Do I need to throw in a load of laundry? Has the cat's litter box been cleaned? Maybe I'll just do these dishes first.* These are my go-to procrastination tasks because they give me the immediate gratification I crave. Handling the two remaining pieces of paper on my desk couldn't offer immediate bliss, so I decided to compromise. I'd spend my five-minute break between POM rounds putting in some laundry.

I threw a load into the washing machine and returned to my desk. I slumped in the chair, wanting to do anything but address those papers. So I pulled out my trusty journal and wrote at the top of the page: "What is going on?" I could always count on my journal to help me find the root of my procrastination (something I recommend to everyone).

As I wrote everything that came to mind, I realized I was jumping ahead, particularly with the business idea brainstorm. The next step I planned to take—to take action on each one of the ideas—was too big (these are the unrealistic expectations you read about in Chapter 3). I reminded myself that it was a list of *ideas*, not *action steps*.

Whenever I'm struggling to make progress, I go back to my supersmall steps. I could begin by reviewing the list and crossing out anything that no longer resonated. Then I could transfer the ideas to my master list on my computer. It was a start. More importantly, it was doable. I spent the next POM round getting that done. I finished by setting a reminder on my phone to review my master list the following week.

Done. I was totally crushing this stack of papers! There was just one left—the quote from the vet. Piece of cake. I just had to call and make the appointment.

I froze. My mind was bouncing all over the place. I didn't feel ready to make an appointment. But why? Well, it was an expensive procedure. It wasn't technically required, although my cat, Kaia, was showing the first signs of gum disease. Did she really need it? I hated the thought of her under anesthesia.

Clearly, making the appointment wasn't the next step. I hung out with my fear for a bit and listened to what Little Kerri needed. I closed my eyes and checked in with her using one of my go-to prompts: "Right now I need _____." I let my inner voice fill in the blank, then I sat back and listened.

*Right now, I need more information about the procedure, how they plan to keep Kaia safe, and whether it's truly necessary or not.*

I compiled a list of questions for the vet and visited the office to get my answers. I was not comfortable with just a phone call. I wanted the doctor's full attention.

I met with the veterinarian, and she patiently addressed all my concerns and questions. I felt heard, reassured, and informed. So much so that I made the appointment before I left. Kaia's teeth cleaning went off without a hitch, and she's a happier kitty for it.

I often think back to those months when I avoided the stack of papers. At the time, I wrote it off as procrastinating as usual or being too busy to start. Instead, perhaps I was expecting myself to take too large of a leap or I wasn't honoring my soul's callout for some extra love and guidance. Maybe it was a combination of both. This is what it's like when you give space to your resistance, when you listen to her instead of ignoring her, and when you honor her needs as she steps outside of her comfort zone. She'll feel more prepared to go through with the bigger pieces of the process.

## WHAT'S TRIPPING YOU UP?

Just as there was for me with my pile, there's something holding you back from completing your work. So how do you figure out what's going on in your piles? You dig in. You want to stir the pot to wake up the energy and invite it to share what it's been trying to tell you.

Below is my tried-and-true method for sorting paperwork even when you are resisting it big time. Before you begin, grab your journal or a notebook. You'll want to have one on hand for this.

*Phase I*

**Step 1:** Choose one stack, box, bin, or folder.

**Step 2:** Sort the contents into two piles and two piles only:

- **Keep**
- **Recycle/Shred**

Any time you're distracted by reading one of the papers or figuring out if you still need it, stop and put it in the **Keep** pile.

**Step 3:** Pause for a minute and jot down how you're feeling and what you're thinking. Do you feel any tension in your body? Are you tempted to abandon the task for something else? What stories are you telling yourself as you sort? Noticing and noting what's going on for you in your body and mind will give you clues to finding the core clutter under the stacks.

**Step 4:** Once you have completed this initial sort, get rid of the **Recycle/Shred** pile right away. Do what you have to do to make it happen.

**Step 5:** Take a minute and revel in your success thus far. This step is more important than you might think. You are cheering on your resistance, and she loves praise!

If this is all you have the energy for right now, wrap up by scheduling the next time you'll continue. If you're feeling in the zone and motivated, carry on, and move on to Phase II.

*Phase II*

**Step 1:** Sort your newly created **Keep** pile into three categories:

- **File:** This is exactly what you're thinking. Anything you know for certain that you need to keep goes into this pile. These are items you'll file for record-keeping purposes. Nothing that requires action on your part gets filed. Only those papers whose loop is completely closed go in this pile.

- **Follow up:** With these papers, the ball is in your court. Their progress is dependent on your next move. This might be a phone call you need to make, a document you need to sign, or a photo you want to frame.

- **Figure out:** This stack includes anything you don't have any idea what to do with. You don't know if it's worth filing or following up on. You don't even know what the next step is! It's okay. Add it to the pile.

**Step 2:** Pause again and note how you're feeling as you complete this deeper sort. Do your shoulders feel tight? Are you clenching your jaw? Is your stomach doing flips? Whatever it is, write it down. Then, take another minute and revel in your success once again. You're doing great!

**Step 3:** Set aside some time to read over what you wrote during your sorting. This is an important step in uncovering the message in the mess, so don't skip it!

As you review how you were feeling both physically and emotionally, look for any indication of the three core causes of clutter: unrealistic expectations, limiting beliefs, or a need for boundaries. Is there a voice inside saying you're not smart enough to figure out those tax documents? Do you need to tell your sister that she'll have to find someone else to edit her resume? Do you think you have to do all three years of back taxes at once?

To help prevent stacks of paper from piling back up in the future, tend to this deeper clutter so your soul won't need to get your attention in such a loud way again. While this doesn't mean you'll never have paperwork to sort again, you will be able to nip it in the bud next time!

Now is a good time for a longer break. You've made awesome progress on your paperwork thus far. Your next steps will take more brainpower, so you'll want to be fresh and ready.

*Phase III*

**Step 1:** Now it's time to go through the three piles you've created (File, Follow up, and Figure out) and handle the pieces of paper in each. You'll want to use the Pomodoro technique here (25-minute timed rounds). It will likely take several rounds for each pile, so you may want to focus on one and see it through to the end before moving on to the next. On the other hand, if variety is more your style, you can do a couple rounds on one, then a couple on another, jumping around a bit to keep it interesting. Just be mindful of not using this as a stall tactic!

Choose which of the three piles you'll start with. There's no right or wrong answer here. Pick the one you feel called to first. Here are some quick tips to get you started on each:

- Before diving into your **File** pile, take a few minutes to evaluate your filing system. Do you have one? If so, do you need to clear out some old files to make space for the new? For example, each year I shred my oldest tax documents before filing the current year's.

  Do you prefer physical files or electronic? If you'd like to move toward paperless filing, there are several great apps for your smartphone that will scan documents, or you can use an all-in-one printer/scanner. A quick internet search will offer several options.

  If opting for paper files, to make handling your **File** pile a bit more fun (maybe this is just my geeky self), use a label maker to name files. It makes everything look so pretty and easy to find.

- When tackling the **Follow up** category, to get the ball rolling, identify what you need to do with it to get it into the **File** pile and write the step at the top of each page. At this stage, don't worry about taking the action unless it's quick. Instead, just focus on identifying the next move.

- As you take on the **Figure out** stack, write questions you have about any particular sheet at the top or on a sticky note. This might be things like "Do I need to keep this? Ask the accountant," or "What does this even mean? Ask Google."

POM round by POM round, keep chipping away. Remember to keep your expectations realistic. The contents of these piles may require a lot of emotional energy and mental bandwidth to go through, so be sure to treat yourself kindly as you proceed.

---

## CASE STUDY: CHARLOTTE

My client Charlotte found some unexpected blocks under her incomplete tax returns. She hadn't filed for the last five years. She had shoeboxes and folders full of receipts, payroll forms, and investment statements. There were stacks of she-didn't-know-what on her dining room table. Naturally, she felt a bit overwhelmed.

To get her started, I encouraged Charlotte to go on a treasure hunt, looking only for those papers that she knew she could get rid of: junk mail, catalogs, random notes, etc. When you have something concrete to look for, it makes it easier to begin.

"Pick one small pile and sort it. If you come across anything related to a tax return, set it aside and carry on with the other papers. How does that sound?"

"It sounds easy enough," Charlotte said, "but what if it's all or mostly tax papers?" Her tone of voice told me that she was truly terrified at the idea of coming across tax documents.

"Then you set all or most of it aside and move on. While we're together on this call, let's imagine you're sorting a pile. You find a mortgage statement. Tune in to your body and tell me—"

"I feel a heaviness in my chest. Like I can't take a deep breath," Charlotte chimed in.

"Okay," I said. "I want you to close your eyes and picture a peaceful scene. It might be the beach, the woods, or your daughter's face. Whatever makes you smile. Take a couple of breaths as you visualize it."

"I'm imagining my daughter running at the beach, playing in the waves." I heard the lightness return to her voice.

"Great. Hang out there for a moment. See her frolicking and laughing?"

After a brief silence, Charlotte took a beautiful, deep breath. "I feel so much better. I had to remind myself why I was upset to begin with!"

We spent some time talking about the importance of self-soothing and taking exceptional care of herself. She felt fully present again. Now we had to confront the problem.

"I want to take you back to that beach with your daughter," I said to Charlotte. "Imagine that she sees something scary in the water and comes running over to you, trembling. What do you do?"

"I hold her tight and tell her there's nothing to be scared of," she said. "That I'm right there with her and I'll keep her safe."

"Bingo," I replied. "And that's exactly what you just did for yourself a few minutes ago. See how capable you are of taking care of yourself when you're scared? You can do the same as you dig into the piles of papers."

As we delved deeper into our work, I learned that anything tax-related rattled Charlotte because her ex-husband had been charged with tax evasion. Charlotte was almost found guilty as well, by no fault of her own. She had surrendered all financial responsibility to him, as she trusted him and believed she wasn't smart enough to handle that stuff anyway.

"Even if I wanted to collect my papers for the accountant, I wouldn't know what to look for. I don't know what she needs and what she doesn't," Charlotte said. "That's how clueless I am."

"Do you know how to speak German?" I asked.

"No?" she said, confused.

"That's pretty clueless, too, right? I mean, why can't you speak German?"

"Um, because I'm not German and I've never been to Germany. Why would I speak German?"

"Well, you didn't get your degree in accounting either, but you're expecting yourself to be a CPA."

Silence. Then, laughter. "Ah, I see what you did there."

Charlotte and I spent several sessions reconditioning her younger self to believe that grown-up Charlotte would always take good care of her. After she got some solid footing under herself, I challenged her to call her accountant and ask what she needed to gather to have her taxes prepared.

"I can do that," she said. "My CPA is a wonderful woman."

Two days later I received a note from Charlotte. She had a lovely (and brief) conversation with her accountant, who sent her a checklist of required documents. She told

Charlotte to bring anything she thought might be even remotely related to her tax return. If they didn't need it, they'd set it aside. If she didn't have something they did need, her accountant would draft up a list of the missing items for her to look for when she got home.

Naturally, Charlotte was relieved after the experience. Not only did she feel much more empowered about getting caught up on her taxes, she'd also chipped away at that old belief that said she wasn't smart enough to handle this.

She was confident that, in the future (and with her accountant's help), she could do this again and that it would be much easier. Afterward, the speed at which Charlotte cleared the paperwork in her house was astonishing. She was fired up, motivated, and more than ready to take back her space—which she did.

---

## PROCRASTINATION AS A FORM OF PROTECTION

While the core clutter of your paperwork might not be the old beliefs that Charlotte or I had going on, there is a reason it's there. Your procrastination is protecting you from something. It's pointing to a deeper, foundational need. The key is figuring out what that "something" is so you can tend to it, heal it, and shift the space from which you're operating.

The issue could be anything. Maybe you don't want to face the pain of filing your divorce papers because they make you feel unlovable or incapable of loving. Maybe if you keep your files strewn about, you won't have to market your business and risk it never taking off. Maybe if you don't open those bills, you never have to face how far behind you've fallen on payments.

By avoiding these items, you can trick yourself into thinking you're sidestepping painful memories, fears of failure or success, and the truth about your financial situation. What you're really doing, however, is convincing yourself that you don't have what it takes to step up to your life. When your fear and resistance is winning, your younger self is running the show. You're likely putting off your clutter clearing because your three-, five-, or eight-year-old self is trying to pay bills and understand grown-up documents. Send her off to play while you—the grown, mature, and resourceful person—take care of this clutter.

Using the approaches in this chapter, look more closely at what you're really avoiding and spend some time on that first. One tool I love to use is Byron Katie's Four Questions.[3] When a thought or an idea you have is keeping you stuck, write it down and ask yourself the following questions about it:

1. Is it true?
2. Can you absolutely know it's true?
3. How do you react when you believe that thought?
4. Who would you be without that thought?

By checking out the story you're telling yourself, you can determine not only if it's true, but also if your fear or trepidation is valid. Further, by imagining who you would be without this story, thought, or fear, you remind yourself of just how magnificent you are.

## THE TURNAROUND

Sue, a member of my online community, firmly believed she'd always be saddled with debt. Using the Four Questions, we unpacked this idea.

I dove right into it. "So, you think you will never be able to get out of debt. Is it true?"

Sue was quick to respond. "Yes! I always owe way more money than I make."

"Can you absolutely know it's true?"

She hesitated. "Not necessarily, I guess. I can't know for sure what the future holds. I could win the lottery or suddenly earn more money."

"How do you react, and what happens, when you believe the thought that you'll never get out of debt?"

"Sometimes I think 'to hell with it' and I'll go buy something new," Sue said. "I'm doomed anyway. Why not enjoy life even more? Other times I feel heavy, hopeless, and defeated."

Now for the big one. "Who would you be without that thought?"

Sue hesitated again. I could see the wheels turning. "If I stopped thinking I'd never get out of debt? I'd feel lighter, hopeful, and excited. I'd be able to dream about my future instead of dread it. I actually feel more alive right now just thinking about it."

After going through the four questions, it was time for the turnaround. The turnaround is the act of voicing the opposite of your limiting belief—in this case, it's Sue telling herself that she can get out of debt (and believing that fact). This gives Sue an opportunity to experience the opposite of her limiting thought and consider if this opposite thought is as true or even truer than the original limiting thought.

Some examples of turnarounds for Sue's limiting belief might be:

- "It's up to me if I remain in debt or break free."
- "I know how to get out of debt."
- "I have what it takes to thrive financially."

Sue's final step was to find at least three specific examples of how each turnaround she came up with was true in her life. Doing so would help to validate (or put legs under) the idea so it could move toward becoming her new, empowering belief.

She remembered times when she helped a friend negotiate a good price when buying a car. Another time, she recalled a larger tax refund than expected and how she used it to pay down a credit card. Finally, Sue told me about when she saved up so much change that it accrued to $250. Individually these may not seem like a big deal, but together, they impacted Sue in a profound way. She realized she's more financially savvy than she gave herself credit for, and now, even though her current debt situation hasn't changed, she feels ready to flip the script.

You can do the same. By facing your resistance head on and digging into it with curiosity, you can drill down to the core issue while also taking exceptional care of your fear. It's okay to feel that fear—there are few types of clutter more triggering than paperwork.

When you address the core clutter, it becomes that much easier to figure out, set up, and maintain a system to handle and manage your files moving forward. Doing so becomes an effective tool for success instead of something to dread. Knocking out the POM rounds, clearing off those tables, and opening up space for abundance is no longer overwhelming and intimidating. Instead, it becomes an exciting, upward ramp to leveling up your life.

## CHAPTER TAKEAWAYS

- Paperwork represents adult responsibilities such as taxes, bills, marriage, divorce, and more, and therefore is a trigger of old beliefs, making the desire to avoid sorting it that much stronger.

- This clutter has a lot to say about your money mindset, level of self-confidence and self-worth, and your willingness to ask for and receive help. Capture thoughts in your journal as you sort your paperwork. Make space for your fear and resistance. Listen to what it has to say. What beliefs need your attention?

- You can quickly reclaim power from paperwork simply by getting started.

  - Grab a stack and separate them into two piles: 1. Keep and 2. Recycle/Shred.

  - Next, sort the Keep pile into three categories: 1. File, 2. Follow up, and 3. Figure out.

  - Finally, schedule some POM rounds to take action on each.

## CHAPTER 6

# DRAINING RELATIONSHIPS: REPAIR OR REPLACE?

The next common type of clutter is one that far too many of us simply tolerate or settle for—unfulfilling, draining, or toxic relationships. Whether family, friends, co-workers, or spouses, this is an area that can almost always use some fine-tuning, particularly if you want to strengthen your relationship with yourself (and who doesn't?).

When you surround yourself with people who bring you down, dismiss your needs, or take you for granted, you can easily get jaded, resentful, and frustrated. Then not only is your relationship cluttered, but so is your heart and soul, leaving you little to live an inspiring life. Fortunately, there are several effective ways to navigate these dynamics that will help you to either strengthen your relationships or leave behind any you've outgrown.

## CASE STUDY: JULIE

Julie's husband, Mike, is a tinkerer. He likes to work on various projects on the weekends. One day he might be repairing an old radio. Another day you'll find him fixing a chair he picked up at a yard sale.

Their garage is filled with scraps, tools, and half-finished projects. Every time Julie comes home, she feels a weight in her gut as soon as the garage door opens. The piles of wood, metal, and equipment seem to grow by the minute, even if the projects themselves aren't finished.

As she walks through the garage to get into the house, she steps over boxes and bins while looking out for nails and screws. This obstacle course is the way Julie starts and ends her workday, and it becomes more annoying with each attempt. *Will these projects ever end?* she wonders. As frustrated as she is, she bites her tongue so as not to appear like a nag.

However, some of the items have made their way into the house, piling up in the entryway and spilling into the kitchen. What was once a minor inconvenience has now invaded Julie's domain. Still, she grits her teeth and tries to keep her cool, hoping that this is a temporary takeover.

When Mike talks about his projects or shares his excitement about the progress he's making, Julie feigns joy and gives him a half-hearted nod. She's so annoyed by all the junk that she can't bring herself to share in his elation. Instead, she makes passive-aggressive comments like "What are you going to do with that, anyway?" or "Great! Will it be out of the garage soon?" Her remarks deflate Mike's enthusiasm for his hobby.

During our coaching calls, Julie focuses on how badly she wants the stuff gone. She is desperate for ways to make her husband downsize. She often asks me for suggestions on what to say to get him to do what she wants. "When I ask him to clean up, he tells me to worry about my own stuff; that he'll get to his when he's ready. He doesn't care at all about how it affects me."

Therein lies the problem. Julie thinks the issue is Mike's stuff, when in fact it's a combination of things: her building resentment toward her husband, his dismissal of her frustration, the increasing anger between them, her repetitive requests to him to clear out his stuff, and her passive-aggressive comments. It's all clutter. Where do we begin when there is so much to consider?

Because Julie has asked Mike to pare down his projects with no success, it's time to ask for what she really needs: to be heard and understood. To accomplish this, we shift the focus from Mike's tinkering to how it feels when he dismisses her request to clear it out.

Instead of coming at him with, "When are you going to clean up the garage?" I encourage Julie to sit down with Mike and be transparent about what she needs, even if it makes her feel vulnerable. This takes a lot more courage than being snippy. If she is transparent and he still doesn't do anything, she runs the risk of being hurt and disappointed. Alternatively, if he doesn't respond to her nagging at all, she gets to just be angry.

Anger is often a more comfortable emotion than pain. In fact, anger is usually the disguise behind which pain lives. However, unless Julie lets Mike know exactly how his clutter affects her, he's going to think she's just being difficult and unsupportive. Once Julie is honest with him, the game changes. It's not even a game at that point—it's two adults engaging in clean and clear communication.

Together, Julie and I come up with a sample script for her to try:

"Mike, I know how much you love to tinker and work on various projects, and I don't want to squash that desire. However, the amount of supplies and tools and the space they take up makes me feel like I'm suffocating. It stresses me out, and I find myself becoming angry and resentful of you, and I don't want to feel that way. I'd like to put our heads together and come up with a way for you to enjoy your hobbies while also allowing me the space and organization I need to feel calm. What do you say?"

Once we come up with the language, the idea of talking to Mike doesn't feel so scary. In fact, Julie finds herself softening toward him, because her defenses are already dropping.

Though it takes more than one conversation, Julie and Mike eventually find a solution. Mike agrees to keep his projects contained to the garage and to tidy them up when he's finished for the day. Julie agrees to let that area be his domain to do with what he likes, while she reclaims the kitchen as her own. In the end, both are satisfied with the results of their communication and feel better for it.

Julie's willingness to have honest conversations with Mike and Mike's willingness to hear Julie's concerns allow them to drop their charged emotions and really hear one another. As a result, they're handling much more than the physical clutter. They're deepening their relationship at the same time.

---

## IS IT YOU OR THEM?

Relationship clutter? Is that even a real thing? Oh yes, it's a *big* thing! In fact, this type of clutter can be a huge source of dissatisfaction and unhappiness in one's life. Whether you have people around you who drain your energy, or you feel deprived of deep, meaningful friendships, this area of your life plays a huge role in blazing your trail—of leveling up your life. Spend your precious and finite time with those who detract from or even sabotage your vision, and you'll find yourself running in circles playing the "poor me" card.

When it comes to relationship clutter, the cause is almost never what it appears to be. Maybe you think you don't have anyone in your life who supports you but you've never actually asked for help. Maybe you're fed up with people taking advantage of your kindness, but your behavior tells them to expect nothing less of you. Maybe you're tired of being the go-to person for everyone's problems, but you jump at the chance when you're called. There are almost always hidden factors.

**Relationship clutter can show up in any dynamic:**

- Family (spouses, parents, children, siblings, in-laws)
- Work (employers, employees, co-workers)
- Friends
- Neighbors
- And more

To identify where you might have relationship clutter, think about the people in your life. Who do you feel excited to spend time with? Who do you dread getting together with? Who supports and inspires you? Who brings you down or tells you all the ways the world is rotten? Who falls in the middle somewhere?

## WHOSE COMPANY DO YOU KEEP?

Renowned businessman Jim Rohn once made the observation that "You're the average of the five people you spend the most time with." Simplified, this means that your own personality and actions can be summed up by the personalities and actions of those you surround yourself with. A similar concept is "Show me your friends, and I'll show you your future." The types of people with whom you choose to spend your time greatly influence your life, where you're headed, and your likelihood of success.

When you spend time with those who are curious, driven, excited about life, able to handle uncomfortable feelings, and able to have honest and vulnerable conversations, you begin to behave in a similar way, first in their company and then beyond. As a result, you find opportunities increasing and challenges decreasing. On the other side of the coin, when you spend time with those who are negative and toxic, you begin to doubt your own vision. Not only that, but you begin to subscribe to the pessimism. As a result, challenges arise as opportunities disappear.

None of this is a trick or a coincidence. The gifts and opportunities have been there all along, as have the challenges. Your mindset and behavior determine how much of each you see, and your actions determine whether you take advantage of opportunities or let challenges bring you down. This is why it's important to feed your head, heart, and soul with positive relationships—they nourish you and nurture your chances for growth.

Does this mean you have to end every relationship that isn't all kittens and rainbows? Of course not. No relationship, romantic, platonic, or otherwise, is going to be perfect. But this is where the real work begins.

## EVALUATE YOUR PEEPS

When you think about your people, who would you be sad to lose? Who are the ones you wouldn't miss at all? This is the start of the repair/replace approach to relationship clutter. Who is worth putting in the work for and who is a lost cause?

First, think about the people you classified as the "downers" in Chapter 4. Are any of these relationships worthy of repair? This might be a friend who always cancels at the last minute but who, in the past, has supported you through some tough times. Or maybe you've reached a breaking point in your marriage, even if the love you once had still shines through. These are relationships that you're not ready to give up on yet—if only the mess between you could be cleaned up, you'd be thrilled to have them in your life.

I've been there. I once had a co-worker who I became close friends with. We'll call him Ron. He was like a brother to me. I loved him and we always looked out for each other. He had come to my rescue on numerous occasions and vice versa. Yet, at the same time, he drove me bonkers. He relied on me way too much for even the simplest of things. I remember one occasion in particular when the office was getting together for a holiday party.

My phone chimed. It was a text from Ron.

"What's the address for the restaurant where we're meeting tonight?" he asked.

I rolled my eyes. I knew he had a smartphone. Why couldn't he just look it up himself?

I was annoyed, but I typed out a reply all the same. "465 West Main Street."

Despite looking forward to the event, I had become annoyed at Ron's helplessness. Although it seems like a simple question, it had just landed at the top of a pile of hundreds of other simple questions over the years. It was the last straw.

I found myself dreading seeing him, whereas only minutes before, I was excited.

This wasn't a friendship I wanted to end. I just didn't want him to default to me whenever he needed something. It was time to retrain him in how to be in a friendship with me.

Admittedly, my boundaries setting didn't start off on the best foot. I took the cowardly way out and behaved passive-aggressively with him. The next time he texted me, he asked, "What time is the game on tonight?" I replied with "Google.com." Realizing that wasn't the most mature way to handle it, I changed things up the next time he asked a similar question and wrote, "Hmm, not sure. Maybe check online." Before long, he got the message (without me having to directly address it) that I wasn't his personal info broker.

This is an example of a silent, or behavioral, boundary. By not engaging in the same way I used to, I let Ron know that things were different now. Had he continued to reach out with simple questions despite my change in behavior, I would have had to talk to him about it.

When he came to me to vent about his wife or a co-worker, instead of offering solutions (in hopes of not only helping him, but also making the situation go away so I didn't have to hear about it anymore) I simply listened. After all, it wasn't my job to fix his situation. In fact, that wasn't even what he wanted. He just needed someone to bounce thoughts and ideas off of. I willingly became that someone.

That said, I did have an internal rule that if he complained about the same thing at least three times, I'd let him know that I was happy to support him in making a change, but that I could no longer be his dumping ground for his frustrations. I wouldn't be doing either of us any good by letting him stay stuck in a negative cycle.

Ron struggled a lot in his relationship with our boss and would often come to me to let off steam. Honoring my own boundary, when he brought up the same topic for the third time, I gently drew the line:

"Ron, I care about you, and I hate to see you so angry. While I'm happy to be a sounding board, I'm not doing you any favors by letting you vent only to feel better temporarily. Instead, let's think about what you could say to her to express your frustration in a productive way."

Creating a safe space for Ron to come to when he was aggravated was a nice thing to do, but by lovingly encouraging him to do something about the situation and helping him prepare what to say, I helped him solve the problem altogether. By extension, it caused him to complain to me less often. As a result, Ron felt empowered and I felt less drained. Ultimately, it deepened our friendship.

Fortunately, Ron was receptive to these new dynamics of our relationship. That won't always be the case. There will be times when you address an issue in a relationship and the other person won't budge from their way of doing things. Although this can be challenging, hope is not lost! You needn't change their behavior to be successful. You need only change your own. Eventually, one of two things will happen: they'll get on board or you'll have to reevaluate the relationship.

My dear friend Elaina had been thinking about staying home for Thanksgiving for a few years. She loved the idea of avoiding the stress of traveling and instead hosting a Friendsgiving meal for her local soul family. Every October she'd say the same thing to me: "I'm staying here for Thanksgiving. That's it. I've decided. I know I say this every year, but this year I mean it. Now I just need to let my parents know." Then November would roll around, and she'd inevitably end up calling me from her car, griping about traffic as she traveled to her hometown to eat turkey with her folks and siblings.

"Why didn't you stay home, Elaina?" I'd ask, exasperated.

Her answer was always the same. "I didn't want to disappoint my parents."

Isn't it interesting how we're so afraid of disappointing others while being so quick to disappoint ourselves?

By the time the next year rolled around, Elaina seemed more determined than ever to have her Friendsgiving. I knew this because she started talking to me about it in September instead of October.

"This is the year," she said. "My first annual Friendsgiving instead of going to my parents' house and celebrating with my family."

This was the third time she said this to me, and by now, you know my rule of threes! I was done being a sounding board. It was time for action!

"Great, Elaina! I'm here to support you in making it happen. When are you telling your parents of your plans?"

She was a little taken aback at my question. She was so used to me simply responding with "good for you!"

"Oh, I don't know. Soon, I guess." She sounded insincere and uncertain.

"Is it cool if I put on my coach hat for a minute?" I asked her. I wanted to encourage Elaina to brainstorm what she would say to her parents when she shared the news.

"Sure, go for it."

"You don't need to have the conversation right now, but I think it's important to get the ball rolling. A great starting point could be pinning down exactly what it is that you want to say. Doing so makes it more real and helps you to see it might not be as scary as you think. We can even play with some language now if you'd like."

"I guess it couldn't hurt," Elaina said.

In coming up with what to say, I shared the trick from Chapter 5.

"Short, sweet, and to the point is best," I told her. "Anything more than that and you invite them to challenge your position. Just state the facts concisely."

"That seems a bit cold for talking with my parents," she said. "Don't I owe them an explanation?"

"Sure, give them a reason if you'd like, just do it in a way that shows it's not negotiable. Something like, 'I've decided to stay local this year for Thanksgiving. Traveling at that time of year stresses me out and makes it difficult for me to enjoy it. I hope you understand.'"

"That doesn't sound too scary," Elaina said.

"Great! Sit with it, sleep on it, and see how you feel later."

Elaina felt pretty good at the end of the week and decided to share the news with her parents sooner than later. And it went well! Sure, they were disappointed, but they also understood.

A few days later, Elaina grabbed her phone to text her siblings and let them know. As she looked at the screen, she noticed that she missed a message from her sister, Jennifer.

"What do you mean you're not coming home for Thanksgiving?!" it read. "You'll break Mom and Dad's hearts!"

Whoa. That was a bit of a surprise. Though it really shouldn't have been, since Jennifer was always dramatic.

Elaina texted her back. "I already spoke to them, and they're fine. Yes, they'll miss having me there, but they understand."

"OK, if you say so," her sister texted back.

Elaina called me. "I got an interesting text from Jennifer, and I've been spiraling ever since."

Oh boy. I'd heard of these "interesting" texts before.

"What is she up to now?" I asked.

"She's hinting at the fact that my parents aren't being fully honest with how they feel about me not coming home for Thanksgiving."

Jennifer always pulled this crap. Because she couldn't be open with her feelings, they always came out sideways.

"Elaina, don't play her game. Remember that tip I gave you when dealing with people who lash out? Remind yourself: 'She's not an asshole. She's just wounded.'"

Elaina laughed. "I know. You're right, but I still want to respond to her."

"Great," I said. "Since you're already batting a thousand setting boundaries with family by choosing to stay home for Thanksgiving, let's set another! Tell Jennifer that if there is something else your parents want to tell you, they're welcome to do so, and that you'd appreciate it if she'd leave it at that."

"Oh, she'll never 'leave it at that,'" Elaina said.

"She'll have to if you keep reminding her," I said.

And that's just what Elaina did. Any time her sister made another comment, Elaina would reset her boundary. "They're welcome to talk with me further about it if they'd like. You don't have to worry about it, Jennifer."

The third time Jennifer made a snarky remark, Elaina beefed up the boundary. "Jennifer, I've asked you not to be a messenger for Mom and Dad. They can talk to me directly if they'd like. Please don't bring this up to me again. If you have feelings about my decision that you'd like to talk about, I'd be happy to, but I'm not discussing Mom and Dad with you again."

Jennifer finally backed down. She was a boundary pusher, but Elaina held her ground. She knew Jennifer was projecting some of her own feelings onto their parents, and while Elaina wanted to invite Jennifer to express her own thoughts, she knew that her sister likely wouldn't.

"She must not be ready to share," Elaina said to me as she beamed with pride over her boundary setting. "I do feel bad, and it's nice to know I'll be missed, but it's time for me to make my desires more of a priority."

"Amen!" I replied. And that was the end of it. Elaina got her Friendsgiving and new boundaries that her family had to respect. A happy ending!

## YOUR NEEDS MATTER

I get it. Sometimes it's not that easy. No one looks forward to disappointing someone they care about. But what about *you*? When you make it a habit to say yes to everyone else and neglect yourself, you're bound to end up with relationship clutter. You'll attract takers, create unbalanced friendships, and let the universe know that you're willing to settle for less.

When your world becomes full of takers, you might find yourself blaming them for your unhappiness, but they're only doing what you've allowed them to for so long. You're likely frustrated or hurt, and pointing fingers is easier than taking a good, hard look at yourself. Even if your spouse, friend, sibling, or parent is demanding and needy, you ultimately get to decide if you're going to participate in the game. Every time you do, you become a part of the clutter— that is, until you decide enough is enough and set boundaries for yourself.

## IS IT TIME TO SAY GOOD-BYE?

Sometimes boundaries aren't enough. Sometimes relationships are not worth repairing. There may come a time when it becomes clear that a relationship has come to a natural end. Other times it may have to be cut off entirely. While it can be difficult to walk away, maintaining such a relationship takes up precious space and energy that could be better used elsewhere. It also gets in the way of deepening the relationships that matter.

## CASE STUDY: ROSA

During our coaching sessions, my client Rosa and I discuss the various kinds of clutter in her life as we work toward her goal of finding a deep, meaningful romantic partner. When I ask her about anyone who brings her down, she immediately mentions Samantha, her childhood friend for over 30 years.

"But we don't need to spend time talking about her," she says. "I rarely see her."

The fact that Rosa is quick to both mention and dismiss Samantha when asked about negative relationships tells me there's something more going on. I ask if she'd be willing to share a little bit more about Samantha.

"She likes to get together more than I do," Rosa says, "and I'm always exhausted after spending time with her because she's so negative. She's like that Debbie Downer character on *Saturday Night Live*. I usually just dodge her phone calls or come up with excuses for why I can't meet up. When I share good news with her, she is quick to tear it down."

This isn't new behavior on Samantha's part. Rosa has simply tolerated it. If she saw Samantha more often, maybe she'd make repairing the relationship more of a priority, but for now, she sucks it up when they're together and recovers during the months they're not.

I remind Rosa that out of sight isn't out of mind. While her friendship with Samantha may not be in her face every day, it is hanging heavy in the back of her mind whether she realizes it or not. There's always a part of her anticipating Samantha's next contact. I encourage Rosa to give some serious thought to this relationship and decide whether it's important enough to repair or whether it has run its course and it's time to say good-bye.

After a few weeks, Rosa says she's going to end the friendship. This is a big step and one she is clearly ready for. We talk about her options for ending it: let it fizzle out by not responding to her messages or by spacing the responses out until they become nil. If Samantha continues reaching out despite the lack of response, then Rosa would need to have a conversation with her.

I suggest some language to Rosa. "You could say something like, 'In honor of our years of friendship, I want to be honest with you. I feel like we've been growing apart for a while now, and while I have valued our time together over the years, I don't have the space to devote to our friendship anymore.'"

Rosa is naturally hesitant because she's afraid Samantha may react poorly or be hurt. I appreciate Rosa's hesitation. Setting a boundary is tricky. You never know how the other person will respond. However—and this can be difficult to accept—it doesn't matter. What matters is that you take care of your needs and let them be known in whatever way feels best to you.

Because she and Samantha communicate mostly by text, I suggest ending the friendship that way. It needn't be in person or on a phone call. It's not cowardly or a cop-out. It's aligned with the way they normally interact and will also allow Rosa to word her message exactly the way she wants without worrying about stumbling verbally. It will also give Samantha time to digest it.

I feel Rosa's energy relax. "That feels like something I could do."

After some more soul searching, Rosa did end her friendship with Samantha. She sent her a brief response to a text inviting her to get together using language similar to what we came up with during our coaching sessions.

Samantha's response was short but stung. "Wow. Okay. Have a good life."

While it was uncomfortable to do and she felt bad after receiving Samantha's reply, Rosa felt a sense of relief, which told her she'd made the right decision. She felt less anxiety when her phone chimed because she didn't have to worry about who was texting her. She also felt more emotionally and energetically available for dating.

---

I'm sure, like Rosa, you have outgrown a relationship in the past or are dealing with that now. You might think your only option is to tolerate it, but just like that stack of paperwork you've been meaning to clean off your desk, it is clutter. When you allow the clutter to remain in your life, you prevent your life from opening up and expanding. You suffocate potential and you reject new opportunities.

Some relationships will be easy to course correct (such as mine with Ron), others will cause waves and require strong reminders (like Elaina and her sister), and some simply need to end (Rosa and Samantha). Other relationships (like Julia and Mike's) require the willingness to address what's really at the core of the clutter. For any and all, however, the place to start is determining if the relationship is worthy of repair at all. You also need to look at the role you have played in the current dynamic. Everyone involved in a relationship contributes in one way or another.

## THE POWER OF THE PAUSE

Knee-jerk reactions are a big cause of emotional and mental clutter. You don't want to be that friend who accepts invitations and then cancels at the last minute (been there, done that), or someone who wants so desperately to be liked that you say yes to every request. A fear of the other person's feelings getting hurt might compel you to immediately agree to something you're on the fence about, when in fact you might not want to go simply because you're tired or you've been running around and need a break. It's your life; you have the right to consider each invitation or request you receive before answering. I call this the Power of the Pause.

By using the Power of the Pause, you can take the time you need to consider the response that suits you best. Most of the time, a few seconds is all that's needed. To practice the pause, simply take a breath when an invitation or request comes your way or when you get triggered. For example:

"Hey, you want to go to dinner tonight?"

Pause.

Check in.

Not excited with the idea? Honor that feeling.

"I'm not available tonight, but let me check my calendar for the next week, and I'll get back to you."

See how easy that is? Give yourself space and time to consider the invitation, and then you'll be able to answer honestly. In this way, you satisfy your own needs and keep the relationship channels between you and the other person clean.

Here's another example: You've been asked to volunteer at your child's school or to take on a community activity at work, but you were planning on taking a day to yourself. Try this response:

"My plate is pretty full right now, so I wouldn't be able to give the event/project/fundraiser the time it deserves. Sorry I can't be of more help."

This doesn't mean you're a bad parent or lazy employee. It simply means what you said—that you wouldn't be able to give it your best. It might feel uncomfortable to decline invitations or requests, but accepting out of guilt or obligation clutters up your spirit and keeps you in the vicious cycle of agreement and self-betrayal. Pausing to check in helps you identify the boundaries you need to set and recognize exactly who you give too much of yourself to. Combine this with language you're comfortable using when declining and you'll no longer fear being caught off guard.

This same approach works great with yourself too. Maybe you're a worrier by nature and something is currently making you uneasy. Take a moment to pause and check with yourself to determine the purpose of your worrying. Is it productive (meaning, there is something you can do to address the concern)? Or is it nonproductive (meaning, you're just spinning your wheels, but there's truly no action you can take to alleviate your anxiety)? If you want to be in charge of your life and continue making strides toward your vision, add the pause to your toolbox.

After all, nothing changes if nothing changes.


## ARE YOU A SPEED BUMP OR A GREEN LIGHT?

If a relationship isn't working for one of you, it isn't working for either of you. By continuing on in a relationship as is, you may think that you're keeping the peace; however, in the big picture, you might be doing more harm than good. Setting a boundary is a gift not only to yourself, but to the other person as well. They may not see it that way when you do it, but ultimately, the stance you take allows each of you to progress on your respective spiritual journeys.

Being the ever-available helper not only exhausts you but likely also enables them. Your assistance may be more of a speed bump on their path than a green light. Step out of the way through setting a boundary and changing your behavior, and you'll both be better for it.

Anytime you perpetuate a dynamic or situation that takes your focus away from what you have deemed the priority in your life, you are benefitting in some way despite thinking otherwise. Just like any other kind of clutter you hang on to, there is a payout to your behavior. If it's not immediately obvious what the payout is, do some digging. You may say you want things to be another way, but your actions have to support that belief. If you want something different, you have to do something different. Otherwise you're just setting yourself up for a life full of clutter.

If Ron's reliance on me bothered me so much, why was I constantly enabling it? To excavate the message in this mess, I pulled out my journal. My brainstorming went something like this:

"Why do I enable Ron?"

- Because it's easier to answer him than deal with his repetitive questions

- Because if I told him how annoying it was, I might hurt his feelings

- What if he asks me why I didn't say anything sooner?

- What if he no longer comes to me with any questions? What will our relationship be like then? Will we still have one?

- Will he still want to be friends even if I don't help him all the time?

- That's what I do. I help people. What's so bad about that?
- Nothing is bad about that except when it's at the expense of myself
- Can I exist in a friendship as someone other than the "fixer" or "hero?" Will people still like me?
- Of course they'll still like me. They like me for me, not for what I do for them. Right? Right??

And on my journaling went, until I came to a realization: my friendship with Ron was one of many that validated an old belief I had that told me I had to earn love, that people won't stick around if they're not benefitting from our relationship in some way, that who I am isn't enough on its own. That was the real clutter that needed tending to—the core clutter, the limiting belief behind the frustrating friendship.

## THE GIFT OF CLUTTER

There is a gift from clutter—yes, a gift! It's a flashing arrow that points to the area of your life that needs work. Anything in your life that makes you feel a bit nutty or drives you completely mad is an indication of something bigger and deeper. It can take some real digging to excavate the source, but sometimes even realizing there is something more at play can be a powerful proponent for change.

Julie didn't want to tell Mike that she felt disrespected when he didn't clean up his projects because that kind of vulnerability was not the norm in their relationship. She took a big risk in being honest. The story she told herself was that she couldn't lay all her cards out on the table because doing so would leave her with no ace up her sleeve.

Elaina hesitated staying home for the holidays because she didn't want to cause waves in the family. Her role had always been the peacekeeper. What would everyone think if she ventured out of those bounds? Who would she be in the family? Would she be exiled? Not spending Thanksgiving with her family of origin meant stretching her confidence muscles and challenging her ability to stand on her own.

Rosa's decision to end her friendship with Samantha went against her thinking that she didn't have that kind of choice. Throughout her whole life, she'd believed she had to do what she "should" do instead of what she wanted to do.

The real clutter under these draining relationships were outdated beliefs that made it difficult to understand why we tolerated the dynamics we did *and* why we couldn't see it any other way. Look closer at any area of your life where you feel dissatisfied or stuck, and you'll find core clutter rumbling underneath. When someone pushes your buttons, there's usually a hidden button you haven't noticed yet.

While there are risks involved in cleaning up relationship clutter, the benefits far outweigh them. Keeping things messy prevents relationships that matter from deepening. It stops you from finding members of your soul family. By sticking with an ill-fitting inner circle, you lower your vibe and limit your growth. On the other hand, fighting for balance and advocating for yourself open up space in your life and make you available for authentic, heart-centered relationships.

## MAYBE YOU LIKE IT MESSY

What if, deep down, you know change is for the best but still choose to settle and keep things as is? By playing it safe you can remain a helpless victim who can't possibly make things better. Again, no shame here. This is simply how our fear shows up sometimes. When you settle, you:

- Get to blame others for your unhappiness
- Don't need to set boundaries
- Can play the "poor me" card
- Don't have to risk making others mad
- Get to be seen as amenable and easygoing

If these are the benefits (and are they really benefits?), then what are the consequences of settling? You get to:

- Surround yourself with people who will remind you that your needs don't matter
- Very rarely experience true joy
- Spend your life chasing the elusive "someday"
- Send a message that you only want the crumbs (and it's the crumbs you shall get)
- End up resentful and pissed off

In addition to the emotional and energetic consequences of settling, relationship clutter can quickly become physical clutter around your home. If you're someone who puts others' needs ahead of your own, your own time is probably secondary, leaving you wiped out. When you feel this way, the last thing you want to do is tend to your environment. You probably come home, plop on the couch, and either numb out or beat yourself up for not doing a better job of cleaning up.

Your physical clutter is a powerful reminder of your lack of self-care. It's a call for help—an alert that it's time to make your needs a priority. And these needs aren't limited to a tidy home. Your external environment is a reflection of your internal environment, so a neglected home speaks to a neglected you. The stuff around you reflects an abandonment of your core desires, hopes, dreams, and vision. After all, how can you feel motivated to make bold moves in your life when your environment is weighing you down?

## GET GOOD AT SAYING NO

I often give clients who are burnt out, frustrated, or tired of feeling pulled in a million directions a challenge: to disappoint at least one person each day for two weeks. This is a little technique I gleaned from Thomas Leonard, the father of coaching, who said, "Never give so much that you can't regenerate within the hour."

On the surface, it may sound intentionally mean or horrendously selfish. However, by keeping your eyes open for opportunities to disappoint, you will notice how many requests for your time that you get. You will also notice how often you say yes without really giving any thought to the invitation or request. The cherry on top is that you get to see that the fears you have about saying no are largely unfounded. Very rarely will people get angry or abandon you or throw a fit. Sure, they might be disappointed, but healthy boundaries won't kill them.

In terms of relationships, your physical clutter represents the boundaries you need to set with the people in your life. It's time to say no, decline invitations, and turn down requests for your time and talents more often. Keep in mind: "No" is a full sentence.

You may also be using your physical clutter as an actual boundary instead of setting one on your own terms. Maybe you think it's easier to live in C.H.A.O.S.* (Can't Have Anyone Over Syndrome)[4] than it is to entertain guests or host events. After all, no one is going to ask to stay at your place if they know it's a mess.

Alternatively, you might hang on to the clutter to keep expectations low—both yours and others. If you got your house in order, what else might you be able to do? What could you possibly do with all of that free time? If anything about that idea scares you, your clutter will be a fantastic scapegoat.

## REMEMBER WHERE YOUR POWER LIES

The only behavior you can control is your own. While it might be tempting to try to manipulate situations to have the outcome be what you want or creatively steer others in a direction that makes you the most comfortable, this is the long way around. Do you get to avoid potentially tricky conversations? Perhaps, but by doing so, you roll the dice on whether you'll get what you need.

The only time you can change someone is when they're in diapers, so it's worth putting on your big girl pants and taking charge of your life. When you do, I guarantee it will expand your world, fan the flames of growth, and open you up to many new and exciting possibilities for an incredible life.

So let's get to work!

**Grab your journal and answer the following questions:**

1. What relationships in my life could use some work?
2. How might I be contributing to their unhealthy dynamic?
3. How can I behave differently to model the types of relationships I want?

Then work through the process outlined in this chapter to determine how you will proceed to strengthen your relationships and eliminate any toxicity that currently clutters your world.

## CHAPTER TAKEAWAYS

- Evaluate the relationships in your life. Which ones inspire you? Which ones excite you? Frustrate you? Drain you?

- Which relationships are worth saving? Which ones are you willing to put in the work for?

- What needs to change in the unfulfilling relationships to make them inspire or excite you?

- Remember to evaluate the most important relationship of all—the one with yourself. How are you treating *you*?

- What beliefs allow you to be mistreated? Do you feel you don't deserve better? Do you believe you must give to get?

- We teach people how to treat us. Start by treating yourself better, and you'll no longer tolerate anything less from others.

- Get clear on your needs and communicate them cleanly. Say what you mean and mean what you say. You can't get mad at people for not meeting expectations they don't know you have for them!

CHAPTER 7

# BOOKS, BOXES, AND BELIEFS IN THE BEDROOM

You open the front door of your home and step inside. There are no shoes strewn on the floor. Only a lovely centerpiece sits on your dining table. Your kitchen counters hold only the things needed for preparing delicious, healthy meals.

No wonder friends and family often comment on how beautiful your home is. Everything has a place, and everything is in its place. That is, until you head into the bedroom.

You embark on the daily obstacle course, navigating around piles of laundry, stepping over the dog bed, and ducking to avoid the corner of the box of donations you've been meaning to drop off for weeks. As you push aside the stack of books and random papers on your dresser, you let out an exasperated sigh. Where did all of this stuff come from?

If only those friends and family who gush about your home could see this room! Your cover would be blown!

Does this sound familiar? If so, it's time to do some serious nurturing of yourself. Clutter piled up in your bedroom is a strong indication that you tend to put your needs at the bottom of the list.

The kitchen is often referred to as the heart of the home. If that's the case, then your bedroom is the soul. It's a sacred space where you go to feel rested, comforted, and serene. It's the sanctuary that holds you after a long day. It's a place where you can be alone, where you can cry in private, and where you can escape when you need a break. It's the spot where you want to feel your entire body exhale as soon as you walk in.

For this to occur, your bedroom must rise up to meet you. When there are clothes strewn about, drawers that are too full to close, or so many knickknacks on your night-stand that you can't find a spot for a glass of water, the room becomes anything but inviting.

While you might spend the least amount of time in this room (when you're awake, anyway), it's what it represents spiritually that makes it more significant than the rest of your home. Regardless of its size, it's the most intimate room. The effects of clutter in there will be felt more deeply than in other areas.

A cluttered bedroom is your soul's way of calling out for more self-care, stronger boundaries, a higher position on your priority list, and some tuning up of your relationships. Whether it's the stacks of books promising you the answer to your money woes, the mountains of clothes your kids have outgrown that you can't seem to part with, or the boxes of photographs you'll go through "someday," the contents of your bedroom can change your outlook on life. The more that gets piled in there, the more your soul gets buried beneath it. On the surface they may appear to be unorganized piles, but the feelings they evoke reinforce the idea that your needs are insignificant. As such, what may start out as an annoyance can quickly morph into frustration and anger, and mostly toward others.

## CASE STUDY: STEPHANIE

My client Stephanie hates getting dressed for the day. She's sick of digging through her dresser drawers and bedroom closet trying to find something to wear. Everything is overstuffed with things she hasn't worn in years. She might love some of the items in there, but they're buried under—you guessed it—clutter. It makes getting dressed every day more and more difficult.

"When I try to find something to wear, I get angry and frustrated," Stephanie says. "In fact, I'm annoyed even before I step into the room because I know what I'm in for."

As someone who is already at odds with her body and appearance, the aggravation she feels when trying to find something to wear only compounds it.

"I think about other clothes I have hidden somewhere and love the idea of wearing something different, but once I go looking for it, I get fed up, grab one of my standard pieces, and head off looking and feeling like crap."

Not only is Stephanie feeling bad about herself, but she also has very little patience these days. She's snapping at her husband and kids and cursing at other drivers. I'm not surprised to hear this, given the condition of her bedroom. She has nowhere to go to feel nurtured. She fantasizes about feeling calm, peaceful, and inspired in her bedroom, but the job ahead of her feels insurmountable. She's exhausted at the idea of getting started.

"When I think of doing even one POM round, it feels like too much," she says. "My shoulders slouch in defeat as I convince myself that tomorrow will be a better day to begin."

Knowing how fed up Stephanie is, I give her a simple exercise that I know she can get on board with.

FROM CLUTTER TO CLARITY

"I bet we can get you started today," I say. "What if I were to ask you to spend fifteen to twenty minutes venting in your journal or a notebook?"

"Just venting?" she asks.

"That's right. I want you to write down the chatter in your head. How do you feel when you think about the clutter in your bedroom? What do you think it will take to get it handled? What do the clothes in there mean to you? How do the stacks of books on the floor make you feel? And so on."

"That I can do. I'm so fed up with it all, I'd be happy to vent!"

With stubborn clutter, the first thing you usually need to clear is your resistance. If you can't get yourself to take any action, then the physical clutter isn't the real issue. There's something else at work. Venting in your journal not only feels good, but it also helps you process your emotions, hold space for your fear, and uncover which of the core causes are involved in the clutter hotspot.

This is exactly what Stephanie does, and during our next coaching call, she tells me about the experience. "It started out as expected—griping and groaning about how sick I am of my bedroom and how I wish I could wave a magic wand and have it cleaned and organized. But when I reread it later, I was surprised by how annoyed I seemed at being the only one who is so bothered by it. I don't think it affects my husband at all. I do so much for him, yet he doesn't seem to care about my needs."

As I listen to Stephanie, I can hear the core clutter causes emerge. She wants to get it all done right away (unrealistic expectations), overgives to others at the expense of herself (boundaries), and doesn't feel understood or supported by the people in her life (beliefs).

I put the unrealistic expectations aside for now because Stephanie is not in a place to get started on a practical level.

Instead, we dive into the clutter of her boundaries and beliefs. It's clear that she isn't making her needs a priority, and if Stephanie doesn't, then no one will.

It's not because people don't care about her, but because her behavior is communicating to them that her needs don't need attention. She is teaching others to treat her the way she treats herself. To combat this, I assign Stephanie the following action steps:

1.  **Complete the Disappointment Challenge** (Intentionally disappoint one person every day for two weeks). This is a great exercise to do for anyone who says yes when they mean no. Doing so will not only reclaim some of Stephanie's time, but it will also shine a light on why she overgives in the first place. And it's okay to start small.

    I offer Stephanie some examples: "When your spouse asks you to make the dinner reservations, decline and ask him to do it instead. Let your kid's school know you're not available to volunteer. Wait twenty-four hours before responding to your friend's text message." While none of these no's are earth-shattering, they will probably rock her world, since she's someone who always says yes. And that's good! We want to shake things up. This information will help uncover those limiting beliefs.

2.  **Practice Asking for Help.** I encouraged Stephanie to talk to her spouse about how their clutter makes her feel and ask him to work with her to devise a plan to get the ball rolling. This accomplishes several important things for Stephanie: she gets to practice asking for help, experience how it feels to receive as well

as give, and welcome in a teammate for the
mission. This act of vulnerability is sure to stir
the limiting belief pot as well. Does she feel
worthy of support? If not, is that why she's been
hesitant to ask for help in the past?

Since she is disappointing people right
now, can she ask for the very thing she is
intentionally not giving?

3. **Identify What Beliefs Were Uncovered.** I
encourage Stephanie to make a list of the beliefs
she discovered while disappointing others and
asking for help so we can work on flipping
them around as described below. Doing so will
change how she behaves in her marriage and
other relationships moving forward.

Both practices will likely feel uncomfortable,
and it's in that discomfort that your soul is
more often heard. What makes her hesitate? I
ask her to jot down her thoughts about it.

Stephanie takes on these challenges like a champ. In
doing so, she realizes that she has a ticker tape of internal
messages telling her all sorts of things: she's supposed to put
others' needs before her own, she should be grateful to even
have a bedroom to mess up, and she shouldn't have purchased all of those clothes to begin with. It's no wonder the
soul of her home is neglected! Her actions and behavior are
driven by beliefs that tell her she isn't worthy of having a
beautiful sanctuary.

---

## DISMANTLE THE OLD BELIEF AND STRENGTHEN THE NEW

There are two approaches you can take to eradicate limiting beliefs in a case like Stephanie's, where you think the problem is the stuff when the real issue is much deeper.

1. **Believe it to see it.** This process revises your internal instruction manual, so it supports the vision you have for your life today. You work on *believing* it first so you can *see* it. This motivates you to change your behavior. As we've discussed, these beliefs are created when you're young, so it's likely you've outgrown most of them (and rightly so).

   To form your new belief so you can see the impact of living this way, work the following steps:

   a. **Identify the belief you'd like to eradicate.** Some examples include:

      - I don't have what it takes.
      - I'm not motivated.
      - I have no willpower.
      - My needs don't matter.
      - I never finish what I start.

   b. **Come up with a powerful, opposite belief of the blocking one that's holding you back.** For the examples given, that would be something like:

      - I have everything I need to succeed.
      - I easily break projects down into manageable steps and take action.

FROM CLUTTER TO CLARITY

- I'm patient and loving with myself as I step out of my comfort zone.

- To be able to care for others, I must care for myself first.

- I easily follow through on the projects and tasks that matter.

c. **Start a belief book.** Once you have your new belief, write it down 10 times before bed, every night, for at least two weeks. You're about to have great access to your subconscious during your sleep, so it's a perfect time to plant this new, positive seed.

d. **Act "as if."** Now that you've been planting the seed for a bit, it's time to begin behaving as if it's true. This will be the validation the new belief needs to take root. Without action, the belief remains an idea. Anytime you find yourself operating from the old belief, stop and pivot to support the new one instead. This can be tricky, so even if you accomplish it 1 time out of 10, that's a huge win!

e. **Repeat as needed.** Whenever you find yourself defaulting to your old belief, revisit steps A–D. It took years to lock your blocking belief in place, so be patient as you work to flip it. The more you do it, the stronger the new belief becomes. At the same time, the old belief crumbles.

2. **See it to believe it.** This approach is the one to use when you're having exceptional difficulty subscribing to your new belief. Any new belief

is unbelievable at first (after all, it's the opposite of the way you've been thinking your whole life), but this approach becomes necessary when your resistance is so stubborn that it prevents you from even entertaining the new idea, let alone acting "as if." In this case, you'll need to *see* it to *believe* it.

You'll need to suspend your disbelief as you take action without being convinced of the benefit. If you can't wrap your head around the idea that cleaning out that drawer will have a great impact in your life, do a POM round and test out the theory. When you do, you'll experience the thrill of progress and will very likely carry your elevated mood into other areas of your life. In this scenario, a behavior change prompts a mindset change, whereas the first approach focuses on a mindset change, prompting a behavior change.

With each 25-minute round you complete, you disprove the old belief telling you that your needs aren't important or that the task is insurmountable, or any other limiting thought that has been stopping you. Schedule time in your calendar for your POM rounds and work the plan. The more you stick to it, the more your resistance believes that you really do want to change. Blow it off, and any progress you've made will be undone.

Regardless of which technique you prefer, the result is the same: your old beliefs will make themselves known, allowing you to work on eradicating them and your clutter.

## A DIFFERENT KIND OF SKELETON IN YOUR CLOSET

Because your clothes have a lot to say about you, deciding what to keep and what to get rid of can be intimidating. Clothes are more than just fabric on your body. They're a reflection of how you show up in the world—how willing you are to stand out and own your power. Clearing out items you no longer love or wear is an opportunity to shed an old version of yourself.

As you go through your drawers and shelves, ask yourself if what's in your closet still represents who you are. Are you hanging on to business clothes from a corporate gig where you no longer work? If so, this could be suffocating your professional success by tying you to the past and taking up the space for new opportunities. Do you have jeans you swear you'll fit into again someday? Your present self might feel judged as a result. Is your wedding dress stored up on the top shelf, even though you've been divorced for years? That doesn't leave much room in your life for new love or deep friendships. Considering your present self in relation to your past clothing will require more active involvement than just thinking about it.

Every now and then, I hold a little fashion show for myself. I try on some of my clothes, pairing things I wouldn't typically put together. I play with new combinations. I put on a bold color. I opt for the chunky necklace instead of the simple one. I then check myself out in the mirror and name three to five things I love about my look. I make sure to go beyond simple comments like "This is a comfortable shirt" or "This jacket is a nice shade of green," and instead challenge myself to say more self-empowering things like "I look damn sexy in this outfit" or "This color really makes my eyes pop." I make sure the compliments are about me (how I look and how I feel) and not about the clothes themselves.

If I feel good about the clothing, I might think harder about keeping it. If something makes me feel crappy, it's probably time for it to go.

This exercise might seem silly. It is! But therein lies its power. It helps you step outside your comfort zone and show the fearful part of you that you have her back. It's also a playful way to recognize any old beliefs or stories that are getting in the way. What is your inner critic saying? What are you telling yourself about how you'll be perceived in the outfit?

Another way to decide what stays and what goes, and to reveal more clues about where you're holding yourself back, is to ask yourself some probing questions. Things like:

- If I saw this in a store today, would I buy it?
- Am I excited at the idea of wearing this all day?
- Do I feel confident in this?
- Does it fit well? Is it comfortable to wear?
- Is this a valuable addition to my wardrobe? Can I mix and match it with other pieces, or is it something I'm waiting to wear until I find the right shoes/pants/earrings to go with it?
- Is this item in my closet because it's something I feel I'm "supposed" to have? Does it fit into my lifestyle? (I'm looking at you, business suit or little black dress.)

These questions are great tools for excavating old beliefs. Don't hold back. Ask these about every piece in your wardrobe.

This doesn't mean you have to throw out everything you own. If you choose to keep some pieces that don't fit at the moment, just be sure you absolutely love them. I have two pairs of pants and two pairs of shorts that I really like but can't wear currently. I have every intention of wearing them when I can. However, I store them in a suitcase and not in my closet. I don't need them taunting me every day! Consider doing the same with clothes you can't wear (yet) but want to keep.

Sometimes it's not a matter of whether it fits or not. Some items are difficult to let go of because they hold sentimental value, you received them as a gift, or because you spent a lot of money on them. All of these obstacles point to deeper clutter that needs your attention.

I had a beautiful blouse that I bought a few years ago. It wasn't a favorite of mine, but I kept it anyway. The practical part of me said to keep it because it was in perfect condition, it was a flattering color on me, and it was a good fit. The problem was that I bought it to wear to my father's wake.

I wore it occasionally, but every time I pulled it from the closet, I was reminded of that day. Strangely enough, there was something about putting it on that made me feel like I was honoring my father. Even though it made me sad to see it in my closet, I wondered if I'd be disrespecting him by getting rid of it.

Logical Kerri said, "Of course not."

Emotional Kerri said, "Yeah, you kind of would be."

Mental gymnastics are very real! It was push-and-pull to the last moment. But after taking time to process my feelings about the shirt, I ultimately decided to let the blouse go. The sadness I attached to it beat out the notion that it was disrespectful to donate (which it wasn't).

As I think back to the experience, I don't miss the blouse at all. In fact, I feel joy at the idea of someone else being happy to have it as part of their wardrobe. Just because it couldn't do that for me doesn't mean it can't for someone else. Might there be some things in your closet that someone else would love to wear?

## BOOKS BRINGING YOU DOWN?

Don't limit these changes and questions to clothing. Just like old clothes holding the promise of reaching your goal weight, books stacked in your bedroom can be another self-defeating source of clutter. What may have started as a hopeful purchase can soon turn into a symbol of regret. You may get a temporary burst of excitement at the idea of reading new books or implementing the advice found within them. But when left unenjoyed, these books become reminders of the money you spent on them, the time you don't have to read for pleasure, or the changes you've been wanting to make but haven't.

Similar to sorting your paperwork, a great way to start working on book clutter is to do an initial sort. Create two piles for the books: Keep and Donate. Put the books you're ready to let go of in the Donate pile. Everything else goes into the Keep stack for now.

Once this sort is done, put the Donate pile aside. This is another good opportunity to practice asking for help. Who might be able to find a place to bring the books and perhaps even drop them off? If you find you're hesitant to rally some support, dig into why that might be. Any time you feel stuck, challenged, or resistant is a powerful invitation to unearth more core causes of clutter. Are you afraid no one will want to help you? Do you not want to be a burden? Have you told yourself that everyone else is too busy with their own lives to make time for you? Remember to pay attention to the stories you tell yourself when you're feeling stuck. They are pointing to love and healing that your soul needs.

Once the Donate pile is set aside or delivered somewhere, it's time to move on to the Keep pile. Break this one down into two stacks: Keep and Maybe. In this round, only those books you know you absolutely, positively want to keep go into the Keep pile. Everything else goes into the Maybe stack.

Your Keep pile can now go to their permanent home. This is not the floor! If you don't have adequate storage for your Keep pile, now is a good time to reevaluate the use of space in your home. Where would it make the most sense for you to put your books? Is it possible to put a bookcase somewhere if there isn't one already? Maybe you want to keep the next two or three books in your "to read" stack in the bedroom.

If choosing the Keep books' home is a more time-consuming job, put this pile aside for now and focus on the Maybe stack.

Go through the Maybe pile one more time to ensure that there aren't any other Keeps or Donates you can identify immediately. Once you've narrowed it down to just those books you're on the fence about, grab some sticky notes and a pen. As you go through this pile, stick a note on each book. Write down one reason to keep it and one reason to donate it. Once you've finished, review each note.

As you look over the reasons you wrote down, look for clues to what is really stopping you from making a decision about the book. Do your notes reference an old story or a belief that is driving your indecision? Play the story out and see how true it is. Perhaps you're wrestling with the decision to get rid of your calligraphy books because it's something you've always been interested in trying.

Maybe you're keeping them because of the promise they hold. However, they've sat on your shelf for years, unopened. Do you tell yourself that you just need to find the time, sit down with the books, and give calligraphy a shot to know for sure? Could you schedule time this week to test this theory? If not, there's a good chance they're not as important to you as you think.

Continue rereading your reasons and challenging them, and you'll get a better idea of which ones you should keep and which ones you can let go. Once you have a solid idea of which ones you can keep and which ones you can donate, you'll also have a better grasp on your core clutter. By pushing yourself to closely examine your reasons for keeping some, you've invited the real issues to speak up, which in this case is usually unrealistic expectations and limiting beliefs. And as a bonus, your room will be that much more organized!

At the end of the day, remember that it's okay to let go of things.

## LOVE YOUR BEDROOM TO LOVE YOURSELF

Whether your clutter consists of clothes, jewelry, books, boxes of photographs, or whatever else you have lying around, how you treat yourself in regard to your bedroom says a lot about how you let others treat you in your life.

Treat your bedroom well to treat yourself well. Making your bed, hanging up your clothes, and removing anything unrelated to this room all contribute to the peaceful serenity you deserve to be surrounded by in this sacred space. Tending to your bedroom is a beautiful act of self-care.

Whatever type of clutter is clogging up your bedroom is there to nudge you to take better care of yourself, including your time, your health, your emotional wellness, and your relationships. Flip those blocking beliefs, set boundaries, and practice saying no more often. You'll find the physical clutter in your bedroom will become much easier to clear. And the emotional and mental clutter will soon follow!

## CHAPTER TAKEAWAYS

- If the kitchen is the heart of the home, the bedroom is the soul.

- Have a fashion show with the items in your wardrobe. Listen to your inner chatter as you look in the mirror. Do you feel confident? Strong? Sexy? Beautiful? If not, let it go!

- Do your clothes represent who you are at your core? Are you hiding behind them? As you inquire, check for any beliefs that tell you it's not safe to shine or stand out.

- Clutter in your bedroom is your soul's way of asking for more self-care, stronger boundaries, a higher position on your priority list, and some tuning up of your most intimate relationships, starting with yourself.

- Practice disappointing people. Say no more often. You'll find that the sky won't fall and your soul will have evidence that she matters too.

- Sometimes you must believe it to see it. Believe that your needs matter, and you'll start to behave as such.

- Treat your bedroom well to treat yourself well. Make your bed. Hang up your clothes. Decorate in a way that rises up to meet you.

## CHAPTER 8

# RELEASING THE WEIGHT OF EMOTIONAL CLUTTER

A s we've covered, not all clutter comes in the form of books, papers, and clothes. The heaviest and often most difficult type of clutter to clear is invisible. You'll never see it, but you'll feel it.

Emotional clutter can manifest as anything from guilt or shame to grudges or regret. While these aren't things you can lay your hands on and sort, you can often find them hidden in other types of clutter, such as physical and relationship clutter.

---

## CASE STUDY: LINDSAY

My client Lindsay was heavy with emotional clutter. She had been holding on to a pair of jogging pants she had bought for her late husband. She wanted him to be warm and cozy, especially when he had to spend time in the hospital (which was often). After he passed away, she took comfort in seeing them and holding them. They made her feel close to him. Until they didn't.

Even though he had been gone for four years, Lindsay had kept his jogging pants in a bag in the closet. She hadn't pulled them out in over a year and was thinking about donating them, but she couldn't bring herself to do it.

"They used to bring me comfort, but now when I look at them, I feel sad," she said. "I still feel bad at the idea of getting rid of them."

"The part of you that feels bad—what does it tell you about your idea to let them go?" I asked.

"That it's disrespectful and uncaring, almost like I'd be throwing away a piece of him."

"Is there any part of you that feels like it would be a relief to let them go?"

"I am a bit ashamed to say it, but yes. Although I feel like I'd be breaking some unspoken code," she said.

"And what code is that?"

"That I'm supposed to be forever devastated and never able to let go of anything of his. That I should cry and mourn and wear black for the rest of my life."

"Wow, those are a lot of rules to follow!" I said. "Who made those up?"

"That's how my mother grieved my father. She was devastated for years and wouldn't get rid of any of his things. And it's how people grieve in the movies," she said with a giggle.

Together, we explored the variety of feelings swirling around in Lindsay's head and heart as she contemplated what to do. I asked her to write a letter to her husband in her journal with the jogging pants as the topic to see what this item of clutter wanted her to know. After all, sometimes jogging pants aren't just jogging pants.

After doing her journaling, Lindsay reported back.

"The pants remind me of the struggles and triumphs of my husband's health journey, of the comfort and love I provided to him, and his frequent lack of appreciation for all I did."

Because her husband felt the safest with her, Lindsay got the brunt of his anger and frustration. She was surprised when her writing turned into venting.

"As immature as it sounds, his grouchiness made me wish I hadn't cared so much. So yes, sometimes looking at these pants makes me resentful."

Through more journaling and coaching sessions, we uncovered that Lindsay felt like she was getting back at her husband in a way by keeping the pants tossed in a bag on the floor of her closet—like she was holding a part of him down, just as he had done to her. "In a strange way," she said, "it felt like sweet revenge. Pathetic, isn't it?"

"It's not pathetic at all. In fact, it's quite telling," I said. "When we don't take care of our needs straight on, we'll find a backward way to do so—a way that's not always the healthiest for us."

Lindsay thought the struggle with getting rid of the pants was the loving memories they held. In reality, she had so much anger tied up in them that it prevented her from letting them go. She was energetically and emotionally tangled up in them. These pants were allowing her rage to fester, which was preventing her from deepening other relationships or ever finding love again. Once she realized this, Lindsay decided to finally let them go. She said her body relaxed so much as a result.

"I had no idea how much tension I was holding."

There was a lot going on within the cotton of those pants! With her willingness to be curious about what they represented, her struggle to let them go allowed Lindsay to access feelings that were buried deep—feelings that she interpreted as sadness and fondness because that's what she thought she was supposed to feel about a departed loved one. The pants acted as a great catalyst for Lindsay to explore other emotions she hadn't realized were there. These emotions were a huge clutter hotspot that got her to the core cause.

---

## IS YOUR INNER CRITIC TELLING THE TRUTH?

Physical clutter has a way of stirring up emotional clutter, and not just the core causes that are at work underneath the items. When there is a sentimental attachment to an object, you'll often come face-to-face with guilt, you'll question your worth, and you might find anger mixed in. As such, emotional clutter can be difficult to clear. It's often hidden beneath any or all three core causes of clutter. It challenges your beliefs, your abilities to set boundaries, and how realistic you are about your ability to avoid hurting or offending anyone during your clutter-clearing pursuit.

As you explore the beliefs that are causing you to keep things you no longer want, listen to what you're telling yourself. You'll likely be surprised at how often childhood messages still play into your behavior today. Do any of these situations feel familiar?

- Were you accused of being an ungrateful kid and you'll be damned if you let that be true?

- Were you taught that the needs and feelings of others are more important than yours? Do you ignore your own needs and do what makes them happy?

- Do you tell yourself it would be disrespectful to get rid of gifts or items that hold or once held sentimental value?

- Does it feel too uncomfortable to go against
  what others think you should do?

Dig even deeper. Take your thinking further by identifying the repercussions you create in your head:

- What would it mean if someone considered you
  ungrateful? Other than it making you feel bad,
  do you believe it would lessen your worth?

- Are you afraid that if you put your needs first,
  the person will no longer like you and choose
  not to speak to you again? Who would you
  be if you took care of yourself first before
  someone else?

- What would happen if you donated or threw
  away that item?

- What would happen if you did something
  different than what people expect of you?

The power of playing out your fears can't be overstated.
Instead of seeing if we're able to move past them or what we
can learn from them, we tend to slam the brakes once we
feel any trepidation. That may seem easier than considering
the issue, but the issue is often the source of the clutter.

I'm certainly guilty of this. A friend of mine gave me
a shawl for my birthday a few years ago. After a while, I
realized I rarely wear it. It simply wasn't my style. I knew
I wanted to let it go, but I was afraid her feelings would
be hurt. My beliefs told me that if I hurt her feelings, she
wouldn't want to be friends anymore. But would she want
me to keep something I don't use or love? I didn't think so.
Then how rational was my fear?

While it was considerate to think of her feelings, I
reminded myself that I'm in charge of my life and that I can
choose to donate something. More importantly, no one ever

had to know. After all, once a gift is given to me, it's mine to do with what I want.

Doesn't that sound so strong and confident? Believe me, it took me time to get there! Little Kerri was worried that I was being rude and careless. Adult Kerri had to swoop in and remind me that choosing to donate this item wouldn't make me a bad person.

You might be wondering, "What if the gift giver asks me about the item and I've already gotten rid of it?" It's a simple question but a scary thought. In fact, it's a huge opportunity to learn how to own your power, affirm your decision, and show your fear that you'll handle the scary stuff.

A succinct response such as "I realized I hadn't worn it in quite some time, so I decided to donate it to give someone else the joy of owning it," is clear, firm, and gracious. The real challenge here is to say nothing more. As we already discussed, overexplaining is a boundary killer. It makes you seem uncertain in your position and open to debating it. Your younger self will want to say more. It's up to your adult self to keep her quiet.

Sentimental items and gifts can be difficult to get rid of, but they are some of the most powerful examples of clutter that can help you uncover the message in the mess. They work quickly too. There aren't many layers to dig through to get to the source. The common feelings of obligation and guilt associated with keeping these items often live just below the surface, giving you an awesome opportunity to work on healing old patterns sooner rather than later.

## LETTING GO OF GUILT

Just like you are learning to redefine clutter, let's do the same with guilt. Remember, it's not all bad and can sometimes be a sign that you're taking good care of yourself. Guilt is such a powerful force because we often confuse it with empathy and shame. While you can understand how someone might feel about you giving away a gift or family heirloom, you're not responsible for their feelings. It's up to them to process how they feel and decide if they want to talk it through with you.

Ask yourself this: Is it more important to avoid upsetting someone than it is for you to open up space in your life for what matters to you? If the answer is yes, then I challenge you to rethink your priorities. After all, whose life are you living? Here's a hint: it shouldn't be theirs.

Holding yourself back to keep others comfortable is a behavior that will infiltrate every area of your life. You'll dream smaller, you'll take fewer risks, and you'll dim your light. This is the recipe for a mediocre life. You clearly want more than that, otherwise you wouldn't have this book in your hands. Obviously, you're not going to go out and intentionally hurt someone, but their reaction to your decision needn't be a reason to keep something. After all, it's not really the item you're holding on to. It's how it benefits you that's prompting you to keep it.

That gift or heirloom is merely acting as a shield, protecting you from uncomfortable feelings. By keeping it, you don't have to feel guilty or ungrateful. You don't have to fear hurting the gift giver or family member's feelings. Instead, you get to hang on to resentment and frustration about keeping something you don't want, and you can live someone else's life.

## JOY AND PAIN—BOTH ARE GOOD!

Hanging on to sentimental items to avoid discomfort or pain never works. In fact, it ends up magnifying those feelings and delaying the inevitable. Instead, let yourself face whatever stirs you up. Process it. Get used to the idea of letting it go. If it's sadness, have a good cry. If it's guilt, unpack it. If it's anger, smash the item against a wall.

Okay, maybe not that last one, but you get the idea. If you go through life trying to protect yourself from the bad stuff that *might* happen, you're also cutting off the good stuff that *will* happen. As author Brené Brown said, "You can't numb those hard feelings without numbing the other affects, our emotions. You cannot selectively numb. So when we numb those, we numb joy, we numb gratitude, we numb happiness."[5]

Sitting with the discomfort instead of avoiding it—while not necessarily enjoyable—is an effective method of self-care. You'll see that these feelings don't consume you like you might think. In fact, you'll find the opposite to be true. The sooner you stop resisting them, the sooner they can be released. Otherwise, instead of you having feelings, your feelings have you.

This benefits you in numerous ways. Your newfound willingness to face your fears will open up a world of opportunity. You'll be less likely to indulge in a vice to numb or compromise your needs. You'll be less inclined to fill your free time with unimportant business to avoid spending time alone. There's nothing like spending some quiet time by yourself to invite feelings to come to the surface.

## YOUR FEELINGS ARE LOVING GUIDES

The more you desensitize yourself to uncomfortable feelings, the more you see them for what they are: essential guideposts on your spiritual path. They help you identify what makes you feel good. More importantly, they help you figure out where you need to work on yourself. After all, if you feel shame where there doesn't need to be any, there's probably clutter to be found there.

Invite these uncomfortable feelings in by asking the hard questions.

- How special is that sentimental item, anyway? You might tell yourself the item is special and meaningful but check that story out.

- Where is this item currently kept? If it's been sitting in a box in your basement for the last five years, it might not mean as much to you as you think. If you don't love the item enough to use or display it, it's likely clutter. If you really do love it, make it a part of your everyday world. The days of saving your china for a special occasion are over. Every day is a special occasion. Once you realize this, you can regularly benefit from the joy it brings you.

- Who would be upset if you got rid of it? Do you feel incapable of defending your decision? If this is the case, look at where else in your life you're playing by the rules of others.

There are, of course, exceptions to this idea. Not everything you keep stored away automatically qualifies as clutter. I have a small box of memories that I only open when I want to reminisce. I love my walks down memory lane, and I find I still love the items in there, but I don't need to show them off every time I have guests over.

For the special things that you keep boxed away, you might be able to find a way to incorporate them into your life if you want. For example, my wife, Melissa, has two pieces in her jewelry box that she never wears and has no intention of wearing. She also has no plans to get rid of them. One is her grandfather's ring, and the other is her grandmother's. Both grandparents have passed away, and she wants to keep their rings as mementos.

Having recently realized that they don't bring her joy while collecting dust in the box, she plans on reaching out to a jewelry designer to have the metals and stones repurposed into something she'd wear, like a bracelet. This way, Melissa will get to enjoy the pieces and think of her grandparents each time she wears them while clearing up the guilt she feels about them sitting untouched. The rings will no longer feel like clutter, and she'll get to release the emotional clutter of guilt as well.

## FORGIVENESS FOR THE WIN!

Emotional clutter can stick around for a long time, particularly when not intentionally dealt with. Some of the most challenging clutter to release is the baggage that you carry with you year after year. Regret, anger, and resentment have so much wrapped up in them that there's no clear formula that will sort them out. However, there are ways of picking them apart into smaller pieces.

To begin the work of unloading this clutter, practice accepting and surrendering, all in the form of forgiveness. To learn to forgive, you must first understand what forgiveness is not. Forgiving someone who hurt or wronged you does *not* mean you think what they did is acceptable. You are *not* pardoning their behavior. In fact, you needn't even tell them that you've forgiven them. This isn't something you do for them. It's about setting you free from the clutches of the past.

You won't forget what happened. You'll still have feelings about it. They just won't rule you anymore. You'll stop spending time wishing the past happened differently. Because you can't go back and change it, you need to figure out how to move on from it.

Releasing this clutter will take a concentrated effort on your part and will likely take longer than deciding whether to keep that shirt or book. Be patient with yourself. You won't do it perfectly, but no matter the result, you will be better for having tried. Give this a go:

1.  Start by going back to the incident. You don't need to linger there for long, but you do need to get back in touch with the feelings that erupted from the experience. Sometimes we distance ourselves from pain out of self-preservation, so much so that it can feel like it was a dream or a different lifetime. To move toward forgiveness, it's important to acknowledge your experience and validate it as tangible and real. Feel whatever it stirs up for you. Consider venting to your journal about it like Lindsay did about her husband's jogging pants.

2.  After you've had some time with these emotions, try to identify the ways the painful experience helped you to grow. What did you discover about yourself from having gone through it? Where did it strengthen you? Maybe you learned to trust your intuition more or to speak up sooner. Maybe you've gotten better at setting boundaries as a result.

3. Once you've done that, pause and take a couple of deep breaths. You'll probably resist this next step. I want you to think of the person who hurt you from a compassionate place. I believe wholeheartedly that no clear-minded person wakes up in the morning and plans to hurt someone in their life. Whoever caused you pain, just like the rest of us, operates from a broken place every now and then. As author Will Bowen writes in his book *Complaint Free Relationships*, "Hurt people hurt people."[6]

A vital aspect of the forgiveness process is to be curious about what could have driven this person to hurt you. Try to put yourself in their shoes. What pain might they have been or be in? What limiting belief were they possibly operating from? Where were they broken?

This is a bigger piece of forgiveness than you might think. When you can look through the lens of compassion for the offender, you can begin to loosen the energetic knot that is tethering you to the past.

This understanding helps to move you out of the middle of the mess and allows you to be on the perimeter looking in, if only for a few moments. It lets you emotionally detach from the pain, and when you do, you can process the experience more mindfully. Does the person's past or circumstance make the pain they cause you a bit more understandable and therefore more forgivable? If you can access this place, close your eyes, put your hand on your heart, and offer them love. This step can be difficult, but it's worth it.

## THE INFINITE GIFTS OF FORGIVENESS

Forgiveness benefits you in myriad ways. It boosts your self-esteem, increases your inner strength, and can reverse any lies you tell yourself that are associated with it, such as "This is all I deserve." It also has the power to decrease anxiety and depression. Sounds like it's worth trying, right?

Many years ago, a long-time friendship of mine ended in a painful way. This person crossed a line, and when I confronted her about it, she denied it, despite my first-hand knowledge that it was true. What I thought could be mended by a mature conversation spiraled into a nasty text exchange where we both said some hurtful things. There was no turning back, and there was nothing to recover. I carried the ensuing anger for a long time.

Since one of my most significant limiting beliefs is that there are consequences for getting too close to people (i.e., share too much and they'll leave), this experience was a huge validator. This friend and I had been extremely close for a long time, and I shared some incredibly private things with her. Unfortunately, these were thrown back in my face during the exchange—further validating the belief.

Forgiving this person was vital in terms of my own growth. I couldn't move on and show up fully to other friendships until I did so. Working through the process I suggested earlier, I thought about what may have driven her behavior. What would make her say such hurtful things? I accessed that place of compassion, both for her and myself, and understood better why things happened the way they did. While I have regret about how I behaved, when these bad feelings flare up, I remind myself that I did the best I could at the time and sweep the hurtful crumbs away.

With all of this in mind, it's important to note that for-giveness isn't just for others. Sometimes the person you need to forgive most is yourself. Everyone makes mistakes, and no matter what you tell yourself, you are a part of "everyone." Just as easily as you mess up, you can forgive yourself. The better at it you become, the bolder the steps you'll take as you continue to blaze your trail.

That's the thing about regret. You can "would've, could've, should've" yourself to death, but it's fruitless. Sure, maybe it would have been smarter to have saved that money instead of buying all of those shoes, taken that trip before it was too late, or even done more to help your friend before he died, but the fact of the matter is that, in that moment, you could not have done anything differently. You weren't then who you are now, even if "then" was five minutes ago. We are always doing the best we can, and to paraphrase Maya Angelou, "When you know better, you do better."

## CHAPTER TAKEAWAYS

- Often the heaviest clutter is the kind you can't see. Guilt, shame, regret—this internal clutter takes up much more space in your life than any piles or stacks.

- Practice sitting with uncomfortable feelings. Instead of trying to prevent or stop them, let them in and feel them. It is both a self-loving and empowering act.

- Practicing the art of forgiveness is a superpower that can set you free from the clutches of the past. Forgiving is not about condoning someone's behavior. You won't forget what happened. You'll still have feelings about it. They just won't rule you anymore.

- With each passing moment, you are someone new. You'll never be who you were nor be now who you will be in the future. Forgive yourself for any past transgressions and do better now.

- Emotional clutter can make clearing physical clutter even more challenging because you might, say, keep a gift you don't love due to feeling guilty about letting it go. Work on the core clutter—any beliefs that stoke that fire—and you'll not only let go of the guilt but the items too.

## CHAPTER 9

# PLAN YOUR WORK AND WORK YOUR PLAN

A common obstacle for most of us with getting anything done is struggling to begin. Too often we're focused on finishing when we should be thinking about how to start. The only way to complete anything is by getting good at getting started, and you need a plan to do so.

As you schedule projects and tasks in the finite amount of time you have each day and week, you're forced to ask yourself, "What's more important here?" and to direct your energy, time, and money accordingly. Without a plan, you can easily get sidetracked by things that seem important in the moment but have little or nothing to do with getting you where you want to be.

Planning helps to keep your resistance in check. If you keep things too loose or ambiguous by saying, for instance, that you'll get your closet organized "this week" instead of being more specific, you'll be much more likely to blow it off. If the task or project doesn't feel like enough of a priority to schedule a time frame for it, your resistance or procrastination will win.

As you begin to implement some structure, your plan will no doubt need some tweaking here and there. Some trial and error is to be expected as you find the way that works best for you. However, after you've set your plan for the day or week, be careful to not change it drastically midway. When planning, your first thinking is your best thinking. You're behaving proactively instead of reactively, so once you've made a plan, trust it.

A friend of mine was training for a road race and went out for a long run. She was doubtful that she'd stick to her running commitment for the day even though she knew it was the right step in getting her ready for the race. She asked her husband to go with her to be her pacesetter. This way, all she had to do was follow behind him and let him set how fast or slow they were running.

Her pacesetting husband essentially was her plan. She still had to do the hard part (the run itself), but the "think work" was taken care of. She just had to put one foot in front of the other, trust the pacesetter (and the plan), and follow it. Even when she was tired, she kept running. Left to her own devices (without a plan or without trusting her pacesetter), she would have stopped and walked a few times. But she didn't. She focused on the doing and ended up having a great run.

That's the power of the plan. Once all the thinking is done and the plan is set out, you only need to worry about putting one foot in front of the other. Doing so also stops the "I should be working on this or I should be working on that" dance because those "shoulds" are being handled by already being scheduled.

Yes, you get to actually enjoy your downtime instead of feeling guilty about it! When you know something is on the docket for another day, you can relieve yourself of thinking about it today.

Business magnate and philanthropist Bill Gates said, "People often overestimate what will happen in the next two years and underestimate what will happen in ten."[7] A plan is your best resource to counteract that tendency and get more done in less time, leaving you fulfilled and replenished.

So let's get to planning, shall we?

1.  Pick a clutter hotspot to work on this week. Make it small and manageable. For example, instead of your bedroom, choose your dresser. If that feels too big, start with a single drawer.

2.  Grab your journal or a notebook and write down anything that comes to mind as you think about your chosen task. You can complain, whine, try to talk yourself out of it, or dream about how great it'll be to open up that space. Reclaim your brain by emptying it so the mental clutter doesn't sabotage your success.

    While your brain is often used as a container, it is, in fact, a brilliant computer. It's a solution-generating machine, and like any computer whose hard drive is loaded down, it can struggle to work optimally. Doing a regular mind dump is an incredibly effective way to clear the mental space so you can have your best thinking at the ready.

    What you capture needn't be only related to the task. It truly can be anything. The goal here is to clear your mind as best as possible.

    Before diving into cleaning my desk, here are some things that made it to the page during my mind dump:

    *I have to email that client.*
    *This desk is a mess. I'm so sick of clearing it off.*
    *My leg is itchy.*

*How can I go paperless?*
*Have the cats eaten lunch?*
See what I mean? Anything and everything.
It needn't be organized or categorized. Heck, it
doesn't even have to be legible!

No significant clutter-clearing progress can
be made when you have too much running
around in your head. You'll struggle to make
decisions, be resourceful, or access creativity—
all things you could very well need as you clear
some clutter.

Keep this journal handy throughout
this process for when you want to note any
thoughts and/or feelings that come up with
your clutter. These notes will provide powerful
information for you as you work to excavate
your core causes of clutter.

3. Now that you have a clean mental slate, draft
   a list of what needs your attention this week.
   Include any commitments or responsibilities,
   both inside and outside of your clutter clearing.
   I usually do this on Sundays, and it takes me
   just about 20 minutes. Here's my exact process:

   Draw a line down the middle of a page, and
   on the left side, write your weekly list—this
   is your task mind dump of what you need to
   handle *this week only*. Be sure this list includes
   work on your clutter hotspot. Then, on the
   right side, list the days of the week with space
   under each to assign tasks.

   Plug in any set appointments you have
   on the books first. Doctor's appointment on
   Monday, phone interview on Wednesday,
   carpool duty on Thursday, etc.

Now look at your list on the left and begin assigning any items that remain to the time slots still available in the list on the right. As you do, estimate how much each task will take to complete. When you do, take these three important factors into account: time, energy, and bandwidth (mental capacity). You may have a free and clear day and plan to get a lot done, but it's unlikely you have eight or more hours of energy and bandwidth to give.

To save your sanity when planning, practice this approach: underpromise and overdeliver. Guess what happens when you do the opposite? You feel overwhelmed! As such, it's a good idea to tack on 15–30 minutes to how long you estimate each task will take.

After you have organized your weekly tasks, identify a game changer for the week. Let's say life throws you a bunch of curveballs and your best-laid plans for the week get blown to bits. Your game changer is one thing that, if completed, would result in some serious progress overall. For me, the game changer was to get the stack of papers on my desk sorted into the three action piles.

You can apply the idea of a game changer to anything. Or you may choose to have one game changer in a few different areas of your life. For example, a clutter-clearing game changer might be a donation run, and a healthy-eating game changer might be a visit to the farmer's market.

Here is an example of my weekly plan:

# Plan for the Week of May 20

| Weekly Mind Dump | Schedule |
|---|---|
| Mail Mom's birthday card | **MONDAY**<br>9 AM—client call |
| Prepare slides for presentation | 10 AM—dentist appointment<br>11:15 AM—drop off donations<br>11:30 AM—mail Mom's birthday card |
| Client calls | 11:45 AM—get car inspected<br>12 PM–2 PM—home for lunch |
| Get car inspected | 2 PM–3 PM—respond to client emails |
| Respond to client emails | **TUESDAY**<br>9 AM—exercise class |
| Sort papers on desk | 10 AM–2 PM—write and format newsletter<br>2 PM—lunch |
| Dentist appointment | 3 PM–4 PM—two POM rounds sorting papers on desk |
| Drop off donations | **WEDNESDAY**<br>9 AM—hike |
| Write newsletter | 10:30 AM–1:30 PM—work on book edits<br>1:30 PM–2:30 PM—lunch |
| Exercise class | 3 PM–4 PM—group coaching session<br>4:30 PM–5 PM—post group coaching replay |
| Work on book edits | |
| | **THURSDAY**<br>8 AM—hike |
| Check in with community members | 9:30 AM—client call<br>10:30 AM–12 PM—work on slides |
| Post group coaching replays | 12 PM–1 PM—lunch<br>1 PM–2 PM—check in with community members<br>2 PM–3 PM—two POM rounds on paper sorting |
| Call Danielle about dinner plans | **FRIDAY**<br>9 AM—Exercise class |
| **GAME CHANGER** | 10:15 AM—call Danielle about dinner plans |
| Get papers on deck sorted into 3F piles (file, follow-up, and figure out) | Remainder of day: tying up loose ends, general cleanup |

While my personal plan looks incredibly regimented and scheduled to the minute, I have included buffer time for each entry. The overall idea is to get a sense of how I can parse out what I need to get done throughout any given week.

There are plenty of times when tasks get rearranged. Perhaps I was on a roll Tuesday and was able knock off a couple of extra things from Thursday's plan. Or maybe one day I wasn't feeling my best and barely got through one or two tasks. Assigning a time for each item, for me, increases my chances of success. Naturally, you'll want to play with this format and find a way that works best for you.

Do your best to focus only on the assigned tasks. No matter what happens in your week, if you do your very best to honor your game changer, not only will you make marked progress on the changes you want to make, but you'll also feed the flames of motivation and inspiration. You'll be surprised how much time you reclaim in your day by not having to stop and think, "Hmm, what else do I need to do?" Just look at your list for the day!

## YOU HAVE TO OFFER MORE THAN L.I.P.S. SERVICE

Now that you have the best-laid plans and you've set yourself up for success with getting started, you might find you're still putting off your clutter clearing. Maybe you've been telling your family and friends about this great new book you got (Psst, that's this book!) that's going to help you solve your clutter issue, but you've yet to work your plan.

When you find that you're talking about doing something more than actually doing it, pause and inquire why. Are you talking about it in an effort to get yourself pumped up to do it, or are you talking about it to get a temporary fix—that excitement of sharing what you're going to do? You know, the whole "I'll start my diet on Monday" mentality. I call this L.I.P.S.—Living in Pursuit syndrome.

You've likely heard the expression, "It's all about the chase." Well, this applies to more than just dating. For example, when I think about taking a big trip somewhere (big = flying), I get caught up in the daydreaming, investigating, and planning. I love to check out different places to stay, sights to see, and any adventures that await me. I get butterflies in my stomach and can't wait to go.

That is, until the departure day gets closer. When my trip is in the future, I'm pretty darn excited about it. As it draws near, less so. I'm a bit of an anxious flyer. (Okay, maybe more than "a bit.") However, I made a commitment to myself long ago that I'd never let my fear of flying stop me from seeing the world.

So how can I be so excited six weeks out from a trip but super anxious when the time comes? Because sometimes it's more thrilling to think about doing something than it is to actually do it.

Maybe you've been talking about getting back into the dating scene. You dream about what it will be like to have a partner again: someone to have dinner with, cuddle on the couch with, lean on when things get tough. You create an online profile for a dating site, and you spend hours scrolling through pictures of potential candidates. You've even favorited some to look at again, but you've yet to initiate a conversation. What if these people aren't all they appear to be? What if they aren't interested in you? Maybe it's better to just keep browsing. That way, you can stay hopeful and positive and not have to risk any disappointment or pain.

While that's an option, it's not one that will ever result in you having what you want in your life, which is a partner. At some point, the dreaming, wishing, and talking will get old, and you'll find yourself alone still. But it is tempting, I know!

It's much more electrifying to think about starting your diet on Monday than actually making healthier choices today.

Or to talk about all the innovative things you're going to do in your business instead of hunkering down and putting in the work.

Or to enthusiastically plan all the logistics of a mind-blowing excursion versus facing your fears and stepping on that plane.

Thinking, planning, and talking about the cool things you're going to do can give you a temporary rush, boosting serotonin, endorphin, and dopamine levels. Collectively, these are known as the "happiness hormones" (even though some are neurotransmitters).

Serotonin boosts your mood, endorphins block pain, and dopamine, the pleasure hormone, is stimulated when you strive toward a goal. When these giddy guys are firing on all cylinders, you get a burst of joy, energy, and motivation.

Talking about dreams and goals can provide such an effective fix that you become used to the immediate gratification of the rush. You talk about your plans over and over but never actually take action. Then, when the conversation is over and you're faced with what you need to do to make them happen, you crash. You need another rush! Better find someone new to whom you can tell your plans. And round and round you go. You get a quick rush, but only consistent action results in long-standing change.

A woman in my membership community, ClutterClear YourLife.com, once asked, "What do I do with the clutter that comes as debt from overbuying, collecting, and retail therapy? I look at the stuff around me, and all I see are dollar signs. Then the credit card bill comes with the interest to pay off, and I feel depressed and ashamed."

This is a powerful question, not only because it speaks to the aftermath of unconscious spending but also because it highlights the layers of clutter.

On the surface, the clutter may appear to be the stuff all around you, also known as physical clutter. Dig one layer down, and under the stuff you'll find guilt and shame, aka emotional clutter. Keep digging, and you'll find debt, aka financial clutter. Excavate some more, and you'll begin to discover the real message in the mess—the reasons behind your unconscious shopping.

Are you using retail therapy to escape? What "fix" are you looking to get from a new purchase? Exploring what you're really shopping for is an important step in identifying a need you can work on fulfilling in a healthier way.

For example, let's say you're feeling stressed and pulled in a million directions, where everyone around you needs you for something. You decide to go wander some stores to get away from it all. You see this cute purse and think how nice it would be to treat yourself. Don't your needs matter too? However, you don't need that purse at all. In fact, you have 12 more at home, 2 that are the exact same color.

You look at the price tag. Ooh! It's on sale! Originally priced at $120, it's now only $70. How can you pass up that deal? (By the way, you're not saving $50; you're spending $70.) Now you're surer than ever that you "must have" this bag.

Is it the bag you really want, or do you want to feel loved? Thought of? Cared for? Do you wish the people in your life were as thoughtful of you as you are of them? I mean, you help everyone. Can't someone help you for a change?

Yes, *you* can help you, and not by buying something that will just add to the clutter at home. You can help you by saying no more often. By asking for what you need from others. By practicing receiving. By reminding yourself that you are loved even when you don't "earn" it by doing things for others. That's what you really need: Love. Reciprocal relationships. Nurturing. Not another purse.

Now imagine what comes with passing up the purse: relief from the credit card debt, money in your account at the end of the month, and the opportunity to deepen relationships with those who matter the most to you (starting with *you*). Wouldn't that feel better than the in-the-moment sense of excitement from buying something new?

I've got news for you, my friend: The quick high of buying a new purse isn't sustainable. You'll get a temporary reprieve from the sadness of what's missing in your life, but you'll always need more to get the same effect. One purse turns into two, which turns into 10 pairs of shoes, which turns into a car you really can't afford. The short-term high is then replaced with shame and regret.

Emotional needs can never be fulfilled by physical items, so the next time you're tempted to buy something new, grab your journal instead. Because you deserve to live intentionally. You deserve to be in charge of your life. You deserve to be filled with deep, authentic happiness. Change your mindset to change your behavior, and that's precisely what you'll get—unbridled joy.

To kick off your clutter-clearing adventure, I challenge you to stop talking and start doing. Even if you spend just 15 minutes getting started, you'll be further along than you are now, and more importantly, you will have begun to excavate your core cause of clutter. As you begin to discover the real obstacles under the pile, you will find that you begin to approach these tasks with curiosity and compassion instead of shame and despair. Wouldn't that be a nice change?

Long-standing change never comes from a self-punitive place. Learning to be compassionate and kind with yourself as you tackle these emotionally loaded projects will be a vital part of your success. The courageous work we've been doing together in this book will be the strong foundation you need to take your life to heights you may have never thought possible. Now go clear that brilliant brain of yours and make a plan!

## CHAPTER 10

# YOUR CLUTTER-CLEARING TRAIL MAP

The clutter hotspot you chose and the plan you created in Chapter 9 is the laboratory in which you will do the work your spirit needs.

Deep down you know if you could just clear the heavier clutter—the doubts, the fears, the beliefs that limit you and hold you back—you'd be able to really soar.

These doubts and fears, the stories you tell yourself, the feeling that you can never be free—this is the clutter under the clutter.

Remember this: your core clutter struggle has everything to do with your mindset. It's about your beliefs. And it's about how they cause your behavior. Change your mindset, and you'll change your behavior.

## KNOW YOUR "WHY"

An important yet often overlooked step in identifyng your deeper clutter is knowing what you want your life to look like and drafting a vision of that ideal life. What would you love to welcome in when there is room? If you didn't spend so much time frustrated with or cleaning up clutter, what would you be doing instead? What would you have your life become?

Knowing this is vital to your success because when you have an actual, tangible goal, you'll be more motivated to step up your game and stay the course when things get tough. Your vision will become an anchor you can reach for if the clutter accumulates or returns.

The idea of crafting this vision can be intimidating, but it needn't be. Like anything else, it's best to start small. While one common method is to write a vision story of your life, it can feel like a huge undertaking. But you don't need to know how you want every aspect of your life to look. Instead, think about how you want to experience your life. Ask:

- What is the essence you crave? In other words, how do you want to feel in your life? Each morning when you wake up, how do you want to greet the day? With calmness? Exuberance? Joy? Groundedness? Clarity?

- What would you like to be doing or experiencing that you're currently not? This might be pursuing a profession, traveling, or dating more often. It can be anything from a passing interest to a hobby to a lifelong passion you've forgotten.

- Who do you want to be in your dream scenario? A philanthropist? A parent? An executive? An activist?

- How do you want to live? How would you go about it? Boldly? Quietly? Peacefully? It's your life to live, and you get to choose your way of living.

- What do you want to be known for? What do you want your loved ones to recognize about you? Your kindness? Your sense of humor? Your professional success? Your values? Your family?

- What kinds of people do you want to be surrounded by? Who inspires you? Deep thinkers? Adventurers? Empaths? Nomads? Spiritual pioneers?

- What kind of life do you want to have lived at ages 30, 50, 70, or 80? This is a big question— think about your goals, your plans, your desires. What do you imagine your life to be like? One of service? Of connection? Of quiet solitude? Adrenaline-filled excitement?

Jot down anything and everything that comes to mind. Let your soul speak without reservation.

## YOUR VISION STATEMENT

As you look at these notes, does a theme emerge? Do your answers give off a certain vibe? Make note of this and use this theme as you create a vision statement—a single sentence, two at most—that sums up your entire vision. In this moment, a short summary will aid you more than a full story. Don't get bogged down in specific benchmarks or goals. That will come later. For now, consider the overall, big picture.

A broad vision statement is something like, "I want my life to be one of adventure, presentness, abundance, and deep, meaningful relationships."

Once you have a draft of a vision statement, compare it to your life as it is now. (Notice the word *draft*. Your goal here is progress, not perfection.) Using the vision statement example I gave earlier, does your life feel adventurous or stagnant? Are you able to enjoy the moment, or is your mind more often in the past or future? Is your life abundant in joy, gratitude, money, and fulfillment? Are you surrounded by your soul family (people who lift you up, support you unconditionally, and challenge your thinking)? Or are you spending more time with naysayers, alarmists, or takers?

The idea here is to dream big and then build the foundation underneath. This exercise is not intended to make you feel crappy about how different your current life looks from your dream vision. Instead, comparing the two will help you identify the clutter that stands in the way of you leveling up your life.

For example, let's say that as a part of your vision, you want to improve your physical health. What is the obvious clutter you'd find in your way? This could be things like sugary snacks in your house, a lack of a meal plan for the week, indulging in treats at the office, commitments that keep you out late affecting your night's sleep, stress, a cluttered bedroom, or a saboteur friend who brings baked goods to your house despite knowing your health goals. Do you see how clutter can come in many forms? It's not just junk food in your pantry.

If your vision alone isn't enough to help you overcome these hurdles, unpack it even further by identifying your "why." Why is your vision important to you? In line with the previous example, why do you want to improve your physical health? Some reasons might be:

- You have a history of heart disease in your family and you want to do your best to avoid it.

- You want to get back into hiking.

- You want to be able to play with your kids or grandkids.

- You are tired of all the aches and pains.

- You want to feel strong again.

Knowing your "why" gives you something to connect with when you're tempted to throw in the towel. When Melissa and I decided to live in a tiny house to support our desire to live more simply, I could never have envisioned the challenges we'd encounter along the journey of building it. Because we started this project before professional tiny house builders were commonplace, we did it ourselves with occasional help from a laborer. A lot went wrong in the process.

Not only were we misled by a contractor about his skills and expertise—resulting in a complete dismantling and rebuilding of the framed house—we had to learn how to do most of the work through YouTube tutorials. The project took much longer than anticipated, and we found ourselves justifying our choices to family, friends, and ourselves far more often than we'd have liked.

It was an experience I'd be happy to never have again, but we stuck it out because our "why" was still relevant. Staying connected to our vision gave us the fortitude we needed to carry on and to address and clear the clutter of unreliable contractors, design hurdles, naysayers, and our own fears and doubts. We had many conversations about giving up, but every time we considered it, we came back to our vision, made sure it was still a fit, and carried on.

If at any time our vision had changed, then the tiny house itself would have been clutter that needed to be tended to. Sometimes visions change, and that's okay. They are not a life sentence. Visions are living, breathing entities that will morph and evolve as you do. In fact, hanging on to an old vision is no different than staying in a relationship you've outgrown, or keeping an old sweater that hasn't fit since high school. It's clutter.

## WHAT IS YOUR RIGHT-SIZED LIFE?

Your right-sized life is one in which you feel clear, focused, and fulfilled as often as possible. It's a life where you're not bogged down managing what's in it—instead, you feel in charge of your time, flexibility, and freedom. It's a life where you are in control of where you're headed. While that may sound like a tall order, think of it this way: when you make your goals a priority and adjust your life accordingly, you become a role model for others by default. It's exciting to think of yourself as a trailblazer, isn't it? It's so badass.

You doing you inspires others to do the same. All you have to worry about is looking ahead and clearing the way. As you do, you'll come across debris that needs to be bushwhacked. This debris is the clutter that stands in the way of your vision, and it will come in forms that might surprise you.

It can be stacks of paperwork that taunt you every day. They might exhaust you while validating the story you tell yourself that you're not to be trusted with important things.

It can be a closet overflowing with clothes you haven't worn in months or years or that no longer represent who you are. It can deflate you as you put on the same uniform you wear every day, the one that allows you to fade into the background of your own life.

It can be an old belief that's been playing in your mind since you were a child, telling you that you don't have what it takes to get it done or that others' needs must come first.

It can be a draining relationship—romantic or otherwise—that exhausts you and makes you feel crappy about yourself.

It can be a lack of knowledge on how to even take the next step.

As overwhelming as all of this sounds, none of it—and I do mean none of it—has the power to stop you in your tracks. Only you can stop yourself. Blaze your own trail. Pull that machete out from your waistband and start swinging (figuratively, of course)!

## PAY ATTENTION TO YOUR INNER CHATTER

How you approach your clutter makes all the difference. Sure, your goal can be to have clean and clear spaces in your home and mind, but what's even more important is listening to what stubborn clutter is trying to tell you. If that stack of paperwork has been sitting there for a while, what chatter comes up for you when you think about tackling it?

There's a good chance your initial thoughts will be "It's going to take forever" or "I don't have any place to put it" or "I don't even want to look at that bill." That's your resistance talking. She's scared. She's looking for you to take her hand and lead the charge. The more you do, the more she'll trust you, and the less she'll get in your way in the future.

You can use your clutter, including your resistance, as a transformative tool to learn about yourself in a profound way. You'll understand why you procrastinate on clearing things or making the changes you want in your life.

I invite you to continue your journey with an open heart and an open mind. Your resistance will, without a doubt, pipe up. She'll tell you that nothing in these pages will make a difference, that this will just be another book you spent money on and did nothing with, or that there's no fixing lazy. Well, guess what? Your resistance is a liar.

Okay, maybe that was a bit harsh. She's not a liar, per se, but she's a frightened child who would be much happier staying in the cluttered world that is her life. She knows how this life works. She knows what to expect. She knows it's safe. If you start clearing things out and making space for some magic, you're going to rock her world. And even if you know for certain that life on the other side of clutter is so much sweeter, she'll need convincing. More than that, she'll need evidence that you'll take her hand and keep her safe as you go.

As you work on blazing your magnificent trail, remember that little Ms. Resistance is right there with you, waiting to say, "I told you so." It's going to be your job to keep her from triggering you, and instead you will get her on your side. She doesn't really want to stay stuck. She just needs to feel safe with you as you play bigger in the world.

To help, here are some trailblazing tips to set you and your resistance up for success:

1. **Schedule time to go back and do or revisit the exercises throughout this book.** I don't know about you, but I've purchased plenty of books in my lifetime in the hopes that one would have a well-kept secret tucked within its pages, or the magic line that would instantly get me to overcome a stubborn obstacle. Sometimes they'd sit on my bookshelf for weeks before

I even opened them, and I would be excited at the answers that awaited me, even without actually reading anything. There was no rush to do so, because as soon as I was ready to be saved, I simply had to pick one up, read a few pages, and watch as my life struggle magically handled itself.

*Spoiler alert: That never happened.*

To experience real change, you need to do the work. To do the work, you have to make it a priority. Treat your weekly schedule like the sacred plan that it is. Do your best to get in the habit of using it. While it will likely take time to solidify the habit, stick with it. If you blow it off, your younger self will see once again that you can't be trusted. She'll continue to squawk and sabotage you until you show her otherwise.

To honor your commitment, plan to read the chapters that stand out to you more than once. Do the exercises more than once. You'll be amazed how differently things land at various times.

2.  **Keep your journal or notebook handy.** Writing is one of those things that everyone does at some point or another. Whether for work, school, pleasure, or just the sake of memory, write. A journal is an excellent place to start. Not only is it where you can complete the exercises, but it is also your private place to capture thoughts, feelings, and fears as they arise. The more you can stay in communication with your inner voice, the more impactful this work will be. It's that voice that will help you identify the core issue under the clutter.

That voice will also try and talk you out of doing anything. You may end up in a tug of war between "let's get this done" and "there's always tomorrow," which is exactly the fight that keeps your clutter in place. Ignore your resistance and it will get louder. Hold space for it and it quiets down.

The goal is to get you both on the same side— to make the two of you a powerful force that tag teams the obstacles and hurdles you encounter.

This is where your journal comes into play. When it's time to get to work and you feel like doing anything but, sit down, grab a pen, and get to writing. Write anything, even if it's "How the heck is writing going to help?" By doing so, you're putting your thoughts out on the table. You're inviting your resistance to the party instead of slamming the door in her face.

When she feels like she's part of the plan, she'll be less afraid and more trusting.

Be gentle. Be patient. Be loving. This is a no-shame game here. The more compassionate you can be toward yourself, the easier the process and the more significant the growth and progress will be. This progress will be easier to remember and reflect on if you write it down.

3. **Just do the very next thing.** Whether it's a table you want to clear, pounds you want to lose, or a toxic relationship you want to end, I bet all you can think about right now is how much you want "it" to be done. Regardless of what *it* is, it's intoxicating to imagine it being over and done with. However, to finish anything, you have to get good at getting started. And more often than not, starting is the hardest part.

A reason we procrastinate is that the task we set out to finish is simply too big. Even if logically it doesn't seem big at all, it might be emotionally huge. And while you might think the fear of failure is what halts your progress, it's more likely the fear of success. You may feel that as long as you keep yourself small and in check, everyone's expectations of you will remain low, and you won't need to grow since you're safe.

The bottom line is if it feels too big, it is too big.

4. **Super small steps for the win!** Remember, Future You loves the idea of being done. She sees the value in having done it, and she knows you'll be better off for it. She relishes the free time she has because of the cleanup. But Present You is the one who has to do the heavy lifting. She's the one that works, lays the bricks, builds the foundation of success, and solves problems along the way. She's different from Future You because she likes immediate gratification. She doesn't look back on the work fondly, because she's the one doing it! She can't see the forest for the trees, so you have to keep her motivated when all she wants is to be done. How? Through super small steps.

When you feel stuck, impatient, or overwhelmed, identify one teeny, tiny step you can take to make progress. I'm talking small. Smaller than anything else on your to-do list. It might be 10 minutes of journaling about how frustrated you are or taking three pieces of paper off that stack and deciding whether you need to keep or recycle them. Once that's done, you do another small step. Then another. And then another.

5. **Acknowledge your successes along the way.**
As you make progress in your clutter clearing
journey, make it a point to reflect on your
successes more than your perceived failures.
For example, if your plan is to set a verbal
boundary with someone and instead, you
simply cancel plans, it's still a step in the
right direction. A step in the right direction is
always a win.

Why celebrate if you didn't completely
follow through? Because you took action.
You did something. While this may seem
like a participation trophy, it's necessary
encouragement. It contradicts the belief that
relief and celebrations only come at the finish
line. With encouragement, the part of you
that resists doing anything will see that your
expectations are realistic and that success is in
the action, not the outcome.

It takes time and finesse to get your
resistance on your side. Acknowledging small
wins along the way motivates you to keep
going. Give yourself a pat on the back when
you say no to someone's request, or when you
put that candle back on the store's shelf, or
when you drop those items off at the donation
center. They're little victories, sure, but they're
still exactly that: victories.

We're looking for progress here, not
perfection. Giving yourself permission to do
something instead of everything builds trust
and rapport with your fear and resistance.
You'll need both of their support to get
anything done.

6. **Come back to the here and now.** Whenever
your mind drifts to the notion that "I'll never

get all of this done," pull yourself back to the present. To counteract fear, ask questions that call for the details of the present moment, like "What time is it?" or "What color socks am I wearing?" or "Am I comfortable in this seat?" By asking questions of the now, you will find yourself living in the present instead of a panic-induced, hypothetical future.

Thinking of anything in its entirety is a huge pill to swallow that will frighten anyone. Remind your resistance who's in charge by avoiding that rabbit hole.

Anytime you're feeling overwhelmed, stuck, or frustrated, come back to these six tips. Use them as your trail markers. They'll get you back on track and make the journey more manageable, doable, and at times, even enjoyable!

## YOUR INNER CRITIC

If you struggle to make progress or find yourself fighting against your best interests, it is likely because you're challenging your inner critic. This critic is really good at convincing you to stay in your lane and leave things as they are. When the critic rears her head, you'll need your fiery, trailblazing, warrior self to step up and take charge. You need to show her the way with love and compassion.

As a result of your willingness to go deeper and look within at your soul's clutter, you have invited the beautiful power of the universe to rally around you and support you in your pursuits. Notice any coincidences that arise. Be open to new opportunities, because now that you have the space available, they'll likely come pouring in! And when they do, remind your younger self that you are a fully equipped, kickass team who is ready to take on the world.

## CHAPTER 11

# THE TOOLS TO PREVENT A CLUTTER RESURGENCE

Congratulations! Now that you understand your clutter in a whole new way, you have the power to choose what stays and what goes. The clearing of physical clutter becomes much easier and is less triggering when you've worked on recognizing it for what it really is.

You'll find that sometimes the physical clutter clearing comes first, allowing you to then work on your emotional and mental clutter. However, with stubborn clutter, you'll often need to work on the core clutter first to be able to let the physical clutter go. From there, you're on your way to living your best life!

Throughout this process, you've learned to recognize that when clutter appears in your life, your soul is calling out to get your attention. Whether that clutter is an overflowing bookshelf, a jammed junk drawer, or a toxic relationship, you can use it as a gateway to the deep soul work needed to have a rock-solid foundation from which your life can soar. And soar it will!

So, what comes next?

Well, I have some good news and some bad news. Let's get the bad news out of the way first. Even after you've cleared it, your clutter won't be gone forever. It will return. *But* because of the new tools in your toolbox, you can handle it. And that's the good news! You will now see clutter's appearance as a tap on the shoulder to address your deeper needs—usually those that have fallen by the wayside.

Maybe those stacks of paperwork that used to taunt you every day will return to help you dig even deeper into your money beliefs. They might exhaust you and tell you that you're not to be trusted with important things. Work on that belief. Take it one page at a time, both with the stacks and in your journal.

Maybe your closet is overflowing again and deflating you, causing you to choose that same uniform that allows you to fade into the background of life. Be gentle with your younger self because she is crying out. Inquire as to what she needs. Maybe she's feeling tentative as you step out more and more boldly, and so she's hoping you'll go back to playing small. Listen to her fears and respond with encouragement and love. Remind her how brave she is and that together you can conquer the world!

Maybe the mental clutter is loud again, and it's telling you that you don't have what it takes to get it done or that others' needs must come first. Revisit the Disappointing Challenge to get back in touch with the importance of self-care. The trepidatious part of you will see once again that when you're good, everyone is good. Reassure your Little One that you have her back and you'll take it from here.

Maybe your relationships are starting to drain you and make you feel crappy about yourself again. The universe might very well be challenging your resolve and your commitment to blazing your trail. Tighten up those boundaries.

As overwhelming as all of that may sound, none of it—and I mean *none* of it—has the power to stop you in your tracks. I hope if there's anything you've learned in these pages, it's that *you* are the one in charge of your life and the changes you make in it. Sure, you'll want to challenge yourself when you're shaky, but no bullying allowed. And celebrate *all* the wins—big and small.

Your soul-searching muscles are now primed and ready to go. Such clarity will allow you to avoid an overabundance of clutter, focus on the message in the mess, and address it accordingly. While it's possible (and likely) that you will react to the return of clutter with frustration, feelings of defeat, or the urge to beat yourself up for letting it reappear, that's part of the process. Feel these emotions. Hold space for them by sitting quietly with your eyes closed and taking some deep breaths, or by grabbing your journal and pouring your thoughts onto the page.

Remember, this is a no-shame game. The first things you need to clear are your mind and resistance, and journaling and deep breathing are great ways to do that.

As adept as you now are at handling recurring clutter, you're also prepared to be exceptionally selective about what you invite into this new space. Have a discerning eye about what is and isn't worthy of a spot in your life moving forward. Look back at the vision you crafted in Chapter 10. That is your blueprint. It will morph and change over time (as it should), but use it as a guide to determine what to let in. Your time, space, energy, and bandwidth are finite. There are only 24 hours in a day, roughly 730 hours in a month, and 8,760 hours in a year. Make them count.

There is only room for so much on your journey, and these slots are reserved for the best candidates. The space you create is sacred and needs to be treated as such. Instead of filling it back up with clutter, reserve it for the thoughts, things, and people that support and are aligned with the highest vision you have for your life.

This is easier to do when you're clear on your "why," because knowing where you're headed and why it's important helps you be more selective about what you will and won't tolerate. If you try to shoehorn everyone and everything in, your life will erupt in clutter in your home, in your head, and in your heart.

Of course, knowing this is only half the battle. It's the work you do with this knowledge that makes the difference in your life. Reversing limiting beliefs, setting boundaries, and being realistic in your expectations are all vital components in a fulfilling life. If any part of doing that work feels intimidating enough that you avoid it, not only will past clutter return, but you might create more in an effort to avoid the deep work.

You want to be sure you are not creating "convenient clutter." This is when you fill your time and space with noise: insignificant actions that don't contribute to your vision. If you're cramming your calendar, closet, or consciousness with things and commitments that distract or take away from the trail you want to blaze, it's worth asking why.

Whenever clients tell me they don't have time for their goals, the first thing I want to know is what they are making time for and why. Starting here is the fastest way to get to the real issue, because it's never about a lack of time. It's always something taking up their time—more often than not, it's something that can be removed.

When you figure out what your clutter wants you to know and why you might be using it to stay stuck, you can then find ways to heal and nurture those deeper needs. From there, you don't have to use clutter as a crutch anymore. You become much more selective about what or who you let in—only the best friends, the best fitting and feeling wardrobe, and the best thoughts will do.

Those 24 hours in the day may feel like they're never enough, but I promise they are. It's all in how you use them. As you review the vision you've created, ask yourself: Are you spending your time on things that support it, or are you busying yourself with convenient clutter? How much time do you spend on things you don't care about or with people you'd rather not be with?

As you ponder these questions, you may face difficulty in coming to terms with the answers. To that, I ask this: What would you tell a friend or loved one who was doing the same thing? What would you say to someone you've heard say again and again how much she wants to improve her life, only to not do anything about it? Offer the same advice to yourself.

Of course, we all have things we simply have to do, but upon closer inspection, I bet you're putting some things in the "must" category that don't need to be there. Maybe you're doing things out of habit and routine without pausing to evaluate their importance. If there's something you want to accomplish, but you're treating everything else as more interesting or pressing, then take a closer look at how badly you *really* want it.

Maybe you're intimidated by what your goals entail. Perhaps you're frightened of what accomplishing them could mean. What if you go for it and it's not all you had hoped? What if you fail? What if you're wildly successful and then people expect more from you?

Like a student who doesn't study for a test, you might blame poor results on being unprepared. If you had studied and really applied yourself and still not done well, you'd have to face the pain of perceived "failure." Or if you had studied and done extremely well, you'd likely be expected to do that again and again. How do you succeed when the pressure keeps rising?

I have days where my goal is to complete specific tasks or projects, but by the end of the day, the hours have gotten away from me. Looking back, I scratch my head and wonder why I chose to do, say, housework instead of writing. (Since when did doing laundry and cleaning dishes become so enticing anyway?)

My decision to do chores is often my way of avoiding an intimidating task. Sure, sometimes I just want to do something that has a clear beginning, middle, and end. I want the satisfaction of completing something in a short period of time, but more often than not, it's a distraction technique.

However, each time I let my resistance win by distracting me, I reinforce a version of my limiting belief that tells me I don't have what it takes to get a job done. When I can take the temptation to distract myself as a sign to break my next step down into a smaller, more doable one, I strengthen my resolve and my productivity muscles. In short, I get shit done.

Think about where you were this time last year. I bet it feels like yesterday. What was a big project you were working on, or wanted to get done but hadn't started yet? What did you do instead of this project? Now compare that project to something you're supposed to be working on now. While you might regret not doing this work sooner (there's that emotional clutter), the two best times to make a positive change in your life are one year ago and today. There's no more waiting for "someday." Someday is *now*.

Maybe you have a hard time saying no because you don't want to disappoint people, or you're afraid they won't like you anymore. Maybe you're trying hard to be who you think you should be instead of who you really are. Maybe you're scared of what people will say about you if you decline an invitation or choose to not volunteer. Have your boundaries ready so you can make room for what matters.

When you fill your days with tasks that have little or nothing to do with the life you want to be living, you send contradictory messages—not only to yourself but to that beautiful universal force that is waiting to support you.

It takes strength and resilience to say what you mean and mean what you say, and to do what you say you're going to do. Doing your best to curate only those things you truly love, need, or use is a bit like deadheading a plant. You get rid of the dying leaves and flowers so the nutrients can be given to the parts that are healthy and thriving. This way, you spend time on the pieces that lift you up instead of trying to heal what is already beyond repair.

Being stuck might be familiar to you, so it will be tempting to return to that stage. Doing what you've always done can often feel safer because it allows your fear to stay in its comfort zone. This is why reversing old beliefs and stepping into uncharted waters is so important. You want to get used to surviving outside of that bubble.

Take a few minutes right now to either review your past week or look at what you have on tap for the upcoming week, and ask yourself the following:

- Is this the best use of my time?
- Do the activities I have planned support my future?
- Will the actions I take move me toward my vision?
- Am I operating from a limiting belief, old story, or fear?

Consider your answers and adjust accordingly. It can be tough to admit that your life isn't the way you want because of your choices, but it can also be incredibly empowering because then you realize that you are the only thing that's standing in your way. And you now have tools you never did before. Tools that will help you understand yourself in a whole new way—a way that is filled with curiosity and intrigue, a way that eradicates shame, a way that helps you to make bolder steps in your life.

You've got to challenge yourself even if it feels scary as hell, because the magic happens in your stretch zone. Feeling the fear and doing it anyway changes you on a cellular level. You literally can never be the person you were before. The more you step out of your comfort zone, the bigger your comfort zone becomes. Then you're willing to take even bigger risks and live at a level you likely before thought impossible.

Everything you imagined in your vision is possible. You simply need the space to be available to show up and take action. If you have trouble finding the time, check your calendar for clutter. Are you spending your time on the things that matter? Do your actions match your intentions? If you're not, you are not making your vision a priority for a reason. How are you talking yourself out of doing the things you need to be doing? That will give you an idea of the core clutter that is calling for your attention.

To keep you on track or to help you correct your course, keep these quick tips in mind:

- Keep your expectations realistic.
- Set those boundaries.
- Flip those beliefs.
- Practice the three S's: Super Small Steps (use the Pomodoro technique as needed).
- Empty your mind often (write down everything that's clogging it up in a notebook).
- Make a plan and work the plan.

- Be insatiably curious about what is going on behind the scenes (which of the three core causes of clutter is present) so you can answer your soul's call as soon as possible.

- Check out the Core Clutter Cheat Sheet at the back of the book for an easy reference and come together with likeminded trailblazers in my online community at ClutterClearYourLife .com. It's there you can continue your learning, be held lovingly accountable, and celebrate and support your fellow spiritual warriors.

As you walk this journey, remember the importance of self-care. The world needs you in your best shape so you can shine. The more fully you show up, the more your essence and your vibration positively impact the world, starting with your life first, then your family's, then your community's, and so on. The ripple effect of the work you're doing reaches far and wide.

Most importantly, go easy on yourself. Remember, long-standing change never comes from a self-punitive place. Your fear and resistance respond best to compassion and encouragement. Meditate, journal, practice deep breathing. Allow for more time to accomplish things than you think you need.

This process is not a one-and-done situation, so I encourage you to use this book as your go-to guide any time you're feeling overwhelmed by clutter or stuck or frozen in your life. Reference the chapters you need to help get you over the current hump. Re-do the exercises, recite the affirmations, and just keep showing up. Your life and your soul need you, and you, my friend, are a trailblazing badass who is ready to step up and step out!

# CORE CLUTTER
# CHEAT SHEET

When you find yourself stuck or procrastinating on clearing an area of your life, use this cheat sheet of common clutter hotspots and their core causes to point you to what's likely calling for your attention.

**Kitchen:** The heart of the home. When stubborn clutter persists here, evaluate your boundaries (Chapter 4) to be sure you're clearly communicating your needs and not overgiving to those closest to you.

**Bedroom:** The soul of the home. Clutter here indicates a lack of self-care. Investigate your beliefs around self-worth (Chapter 3) and how well you protect your time (Chapter 4).

**Office:** The money center. Check out your money mindset to see if there's a fear of success in play. Clutter in your office area speaks to a feeling of safety in staying small, of not claiming your space in the world. Work on your beliefs around standing out, possibility of criticism, and belief in yourself (Chapter 3).

**Garage:** This area relates to possibility. You might find you live with the hope of life magically improving "someday." Items here often represent options and an unwillingness to make decisions (Chapter 3).

**Basement:** This area is clutter's graveyard. When bins, boxes, and random items accumulate here, look to your ties with the past (Chapter 3). Pay attention to any tendency to hold grudges, bite your tongue, and behave from "should" (Chapter 8).

**Relationships:** If you find your circle includes toxic or draining relationships, focus on setting boundaries, strengthening your self-worth, and how deserving you feel of quality connection (Chapters 4 and 6).

**Mind:** Mental clutter is asking you to slow down and take a breath. Keeping a busy mind is an indication of not feeling valued or significant. Work on emptying your brain so you can hear your soul and connect to yourself more deeply (Chapters 8 and 9).

**Body:** Weight clutter speaks to a fear of vulnerability, a fear of standing out, and a belief that your needs aren't as important as everyone else's. When you struggle to shed extra pounds from your body, look to your expectations (Chapter 2), your beliefs (Chapter 3), and your boundaries (Chapter 4).

# ENDNOTES

## Chapter 2

1. Cirillo, F. 2019. Do more and have fun with time management. Retrieved from https://francescocirillo.com/pages/pomodoro-technique.

## Chapter 3

2. Robbins, Tony. *Awaken the Giant Within*. (United States: Simon & Schuster, 1992), 693.

## Chapter 5

3. Katie, B. 2020. The work is a practice. Retrieved from https://thework.com/instruction-the-work-byron-katie/.

## Chapter 6

4. Cilley, M. What is flylady? Retrieved from http://www.flylady.net/d/what-is-flylady/.

## Chapter 8

5. Brown, B. *The Gifts of Imperfection*. (United States: Hazelden Publishing, 2010), 70.

6. Bowen, W. *Complaint Free Relationships*. (United States: Harmony Publishing, 2009).

## Chapter 9

7. Gates, Bill, Rinearson, Peter, Myhryold, Nathan. *The Road Ahead*. (United Kingdom: Penguin, 1996), 316.

# ACKNOWLEDGMENTS

This book would not be in the world had it not been for my amazingly supportive and endlessly patient wife, Melissa. Thank you for taking care of every other area of our life so I could write, for gently pushing me when I would drag my feet, and for not giving up on me when my scrambling drove you nuts. You are one of a kind, and I'm glad you're all mine. Love you mad craze.

Thank you to my sister, Donna, for our brainstorming walks, the limitless supply of iced teas, and your willingness to do whatever it takes to up my chances of book-writing success. I love and appreciate you.

Thank you to my mother for always making me feel like I can do anything and for cheering me along as I soar and stumble. You are such a pillar in my life.

Thank you to my Daddio up in Heaven for all of the cardinal visits outside my window as I wrote, and for the taps on the window to be sure I saw you.

Thank you to my family, Cheryl, Michael, Steven, Janice, Tom, Lisa, Walter, Michelle, Mark, Riv, and Karen for always being the loudest members of my cheering squad. I love you all.

Thank you to my in-laws for challenging me to think differently and teaching me that it's okay to toot your own horn. And thanks, Favey, for the pride you always beam my way.

Thank you to all of my nieces and nephews for keeping me young at heart, being interested in the work I do, and giving me hope for the future.

Thank you to my dear friends Debbie and Brett for their encouragement, unwavering support, strategizing prowess, and perspective-shifting magic. To have the two of you in my life as friends and colleagues is such a blessing. I am forever grateful for your love and enthusiasm.

Thank you to Danielle, Dougall, and John for helping keep my head on straight and encouraging me to believe in myself more and more.

Thank you to Caleb Deane for your exceptional editing eye and quick action on this project. You are a star!

Thank you to my editor, Lisa Cheng, for your insight, wise suggestions, and steadfast commitment to this book. You are such a joy to work with. I appreciate you.

Finally, thank you to Hay House Publishing for their support in sharing this work with the world to help people get out from under shame and grab life by the horns.

# ABOUT THE AUTHOR

**K**erri Richardson is the author of *What Your Clutter Is Trying to Tell You* and a trained life coach who helps people identify the trail they want to blaze and bushwhack whatever stands in their way. For more than 18 years, she has worked with thousands of people, helping them to identify and eliminate the clutter in their lives and challenging them to play bigger, shatter expectations, and fulfill their vision. Her work has been featured in *The Wall Street Journal, Boston Magazine, The New York Times, Woman's World*, and *Daily Mail*. You can visit her online at kerririchardson.com.

## Hay House Titles of Related Interest

We hope you enjoyed this Hay House book. If you'd like to receive our online catalog featuring additional information on Hay House books and products, or if you'd like to find out more about the Hay Foundation, please contact:

Hay House, Inc., P.O. Box 5100, Carlsbad, CA 92018-5100
(760) 431-7695 or (800) 654-5126
(760) 431-6948 (fax) or (800) 650-5115 (fax)
www.hayhouse.com® • www.hayfoundation.org

—•—

*Published in Australia by:* Hay House Australia Pty. Ltd.,
18/36 Ralph St., Alexandria NSW 2015
*Phone:* 612-9669-4299 • *Fax:* 612-9669-4144
www.hayhouse.com.au

*Published in the United Kingdom by:* Hay House UK, Ltd.,
The Sixth Floor, Watson House, 54 Baker Street, London W1U 7BU
*Phone:* +44 (0)20 3927 7290 • *Fax:* +44 (0)20 3927 7291
www.hayhouse.co.uk

*Published in India by:* Hay House Publishers India,
Muskaan Complex, Plot No. 3, B-2, Vasant Kunj, New Delhi 110 070
*Phone:* 91-11-4176-1620 • *Fax:* 91-11-4176-1630
www.hayhouse.co.in

—•—

## Access New Knowledge.
## Anytime. Anywhere.

Learn and evolve at your own pace
with the world's leading experts.

www.hayhouseU.com